Touched by His Grace

Published by
Kachere Series,
P.O. Box 1037, Zomba, Malawi
ISBN 99908-76-31-2
Kachere Text no. 20

The Kachere Series is distributed outside Africa by:
African Books Collective Oxford (orders@africanbookscollective.com)
Michigan State University Press East Lansing (msupress@msu.edu)

Layout: Caroline Chihana
Cover Design: Caroline Chihana
Cover Illustration: Inkosi ya Makosi, M'Mbelwa II

Printed by Lightning Source

Touched by His Grace

A Ngoni Story
of Tragedy and Triumph

Masiye Tembo

Kachere Text no. 20
Kachere Series
Zomba
2005

Kachere Series

P.O. Box 1037, Zomba, Malawi
kachere@globemw.net
www.sdnp.org.mw/kachereseries/

This book is part of the Kachere Series, a range of books on religion, culture and society from Malawi. Other Kachere books are:

Yesaya Zerenji Mwasi, *Essential and Paramount Reasons for Working Independently*

Stephen Kauta Msiska, *Golden Buttons: Christianity and Traditional Religion among the Tumbuka*

Patrick Makondesa, *Moyo ndi Utumiki wa Mbusa ndi Mai Muocha wa Providence Industrial Mission*

Silas S. Ncozana, *Sangaya: A Leader in the CCAP Blantyre Synod*

J.C. Chakanza, *Voices of Preachers in Protest: The Ministry of Two Malawian Prophets: Elliot Kamwana and Wilfred Gudu*

Andy G. Khubanyiwa, *Better Days Around the Corner: Restoration of Hope, Self-Confidence and the Desire to Succeed*

Boston Soko, *Nchimi Chikanga: The Battle Against Witchcraft in Malawi*

John McCracken, *Politics and Christianity in Malawi 1875-1940: The Impact of the Livingstonia Mission in the Notyhrtn Province*

Silas S. Ncozana, *The Spirit Dimension in African Christianity : A Pastoral Study Among the Tumbuka People of Northern Malawi*

T Jack Thompson, *Touching the Heart: Xhosa Missionies to Malawi1876-1888*

Margaret Sinclair, *Salt and Light: The Letters of Jack and Mamie Martin in Malawi in 1921-28*

Peter G Forster, *T. Cullen Young: Missionary and Anthropologist*

Orison Ian Mkandawire, *Chiswakata Mkandawire of Livingstonia*

David Mphande, *Nthanthi za Chitonga za Kusambizgiya ndi Kutauliya*

The Kachere Series is the publications arm of the Department of Theology and Religious Studies of the University of Malawi.

Series Editors: J.C. Chakanza, Fulata L. Moyo, F.L. Chingota, Klaus Fiedler, P.A. Kalilombe, Martin Ott, Shareef Mahomed

No matter what it is that brings your hopes down or shatters your dreams and expectations, do not ever stop believing in the Almighty.

It is my unwavering belief that, no matter how badly afflicted with emotional or physical pain mankind is, you can always find healing in the great pharmacy of Scripture.

Acknowledgement

I gladly acknowledge the use of these two books for writing this story: P.E.N. Tendall, History of Central Africa, and James W. Jack, Daybreak in Livingstonia.

Once in a while in most people's lives, one person comes along and makes a whole lot of difference. As a result, lives are known to have been turned around, those lofty peaks that seemed so insurmountable just turned into the lowest rung in the ladder.
Well, I too had such a person.
My granddad.

I owe most of everything I am to this man I loved so dearly and as a token of my gratitude, I would like to share the story of his life and his people with the world.

I would, especially, to the young generation of Ngoni (Zulu) descendants in Malawi, Zambia, Tanzania and Zimbabwe, encourage them to dig for their roots and understand where they came from.

This is my way of sharing the rich history of our forefathers and showing pride in who we really are.

May you be enriched by this experience as you journey back to the 'beginning of time'.

The Northern Region of Malawi is home to about a hundred thousand people of Zulu origin. This is the tribe of my grandparents and ancestors.

It is, however, my sad observation that within the next century, the Zulu (Ngoni) language will gradually fade away and disappear as the older generation of this small African country passes on.

It is my intention, in this book, on the one part, to bring to the attention of the world and my fellow descendants how the Zulu language and culture was exported to this part of Africa.

On the other, I would like to share the true life experience of one remarkable Zulu person who, churned by his unwavering belief in the Almighty God, went through the most trying period in his life and still emerged a victor, an icon for many people within his small community.

This person was my grandfather.

About ninety five percent of this story is true. The rest is mere conjecture of what might have been (taking into cognizance the culture and traditions of the Zulu people at that time). It is up to the reader to discern fact from fiction.

I would also like to thank all the elders at Ekwendeni 1 village who took me in and shared with me their stories.

Special mention goes to Levi Silo, Simeon Jere, Simon Hara, Abishai Lungu, all with whom I shared many a cup of tea.

Also to the Reverend Hara who remained a true friend of my granddad till he died and to my uncle Patrick Mtete, who was headman and shared with me the inside stories of the tribal council.

I would also like to pay special tribute to the most influential teachers I ever had; Mr. Dan Ndlovu Chigaru from Maphisa Primary School and Mr. Molife from Mpopoma High School.

Thank you for the unequalled tutoring, support and perseverance.
To all, those gone before and those still alive, may God bless you and be with you always.

Masiye Tembo

He stood at five feet and ten inches in his shoes and walked with a slight stoop and a faltering gait, sometimes having to depend on his shiny black walking stick for balance. From time to time his breath would change to an asthmatic wheeze and he would be forced to stop and gasp for air, his face changing noticeably as it registered the pain that he felt from within his chest, moaning and groaning, willing the pain to go away.

At times, these episodes seemed to last for an eternity, prompting me to summon the services of the only four by four Nissan Patrol ambulance from Ekwendeni Mission Hospital.

Many is the time that grandpa had been rushed to the hospital after one of these attacks and, as usual, after a few days of hospital care and a course of digoxin, folic acid, and an array of other big and small tablets and a number of subcutaneous injections, his condition would gradually improve and a radiance of some sort would appear on his face.

For a short borrowed time, this man, seemingly reinvigorated, would appear to be totally healthy, devoid of the many health problems that plagued him.

Today, he sat in a leather thong chair on the verandah of his cousin's house while the hired construction workers put finishing touches to his newly built house.

He wore a jovial look on his face, an indication that he probably was feeling better than usual.

Despite several specks of gray in his hair, his looks belied his true age. At seventy-two, he could still put many a young man to shame when it came to physical fitness, health permitting of course.

I had witnessed an incident, two weeks earlier, when he had chased down a young man that had snatched a purse from an old lady as she shopped at the market square. The young man had been quickly taken down, relieved of the purse and eventually handed over to the notorious Malawi Young Pioneers. The over exertion had, however, forced grandpa to be hospitalized.

His wizened face bore the knowledge of the old. On numerous occasions he was invited to sit at the tribal council when there was a matter of great concern and the chief and headman of the village felt they needed his advice.

He sat there, his eyes with that far away look that transverses time, bringing back a great deal of memories, memories of youth and fun, memories of joy and pain, memories of accomplishment and failure.

Yes. This was my grandfather born Nemon Vuyani Gumbo to Mjuma Gumbo and Sizakele Mpande.

Yes, this was the same man that had brought me up just like one of his own sons and had helped shape my life with his Christian values. The only person I loved so much I would have gladly laid down my life for.

I sat across from him and marveled at his resilience, at his ability to bring change to the lives of so many people that had sought counsel with him, at his loving nature that knew no bounds and at his kindness and respect for the other person, young and old.

I coughed slightly so as to draw his attention and bring his wandering mind back to the present moment.

He turned his face and gave me a heart-warming smile. I smiled back at him and prompted him once more to tell me what had really taken place the time he had decided to leave this village and venture a thousand miles away from his family and friends.

"You are very persistent," he said to me, "are you sure you want to know what it was that sent me scurrying all the way to Harare?" he queried. "Yes dad, pleeeaaase," I begged. I do not remember ever calling him granddad at all. Ever since I'd been a little kid I'd always called him daddy. Indeed, I wanted to know everything. I wanted to know what it was that had prompted his hasty departure from this seemingly beautiful and quiet village. I sat there, hoping against hope that today he would succumb to my inquisitive nature and tell me the story that seemed to evoke much painful memories each time I raised the issue. None of my uncles, not even my mother, had been told what had happened here many years ago. I felt it my duty to find out and chronicle all events and keep record of my family's history for the benefit of the many grandchildren that would be born long after he was gone. I knew granddad was dying. Just a few days earlier after he had been discharged from the hospital, I had spoken to the doctor and the picture he had painted had not been good at all. Somehow, I had a feeling that granddad knew too, because, on that day, March 22, 1977, he finally told me the whole gory story. He had been out of hospital only five days and his demeanor was the exact opposite of a terminally ill person. Leaning forward, he beckoned me to come closer and in his deep but soft, lilting Zulu voice, I was taken nearly fifty years back to one particular morning on the banks of the Lunyangwa River.

The faint glow of light to the east signaled the arrival of dawn. The stars in the vast African sky slowly began to disappear. The birds in the trees and in the reeds by the riverside began to chirp and flap their wings as they welcomed the break of day.

The frogs' croaking gradually faded away as the women of the village began to arrive to fetch their morning supply of water.

In the village, about a mile upland, the cattle and goats could be heard mooing and bleating in restlessness in anticipation of being released from the kraals and pens by the loin clothed herd boys.

Down by the banks of the Lunyagwa river, half a mile downstream from where the women could be heard drawing their drinking water, the young men of Ekwendeni village sat on their haunches, huddled together around a fire, discussing the latest piece of gossip that had somehow gotten to the ears of one of them. It was alleged, one young man said, that a woman from the village of Emazinyeni, just across the river on the other side, had been caught red handed as she raided a grave site. She had exhumed a recently buried body of a small child.

How fast news traveled in the African jungle.

The messengers had already been to see Chief *Yohane Jere* before first light and had briefed him on the incident. The chief had then ordered that the woman be brought to court at high noon when all members of his judicial council would be present.

Nemon, crouched amongst the other young men, all with loin clothes dropping down between their legs and covering their manhood, shuddered at the thought of what fate the Privy Council would bestow on this "evil woman."

His girlfriend Jenara lived in the same village as this woman and he wondered if she might know who the accused was. Hopefully it was not any of her relatives for that would really complicate their relationship.

Jenara lived with her foster parents. This Saturday, when all farming duties were put aside early, Nemon had planned to go calling on her and had arranged with his best friend Aramson to accompany him as custom demanded. Laying down his axe, he stripped off his sole piece of clothing and waded into the beckoning waters of the river for his daily morning bath. Aramson joined him in the water and asked if they would still proceed as previously arranged following the said events.

"I suppose we will have to go in the evening after court is over", Nemon replied as he took a deep breath and submerged into the water, swimming for about half a minute before erupting out twenty yards upstream.

They lathered themselves with some blue washing soap that they had cut from a full length bar purchased from the mission station. The soap had no brand name as it was made locally by the missionary sisters from Scotland. Worth a *tickey*, the soap served both their laundry and bathing needs .

However, the soap had a very short life span. As soon as the other young men realized there was soap available, they all wanted to use it and scrub away their grime accumulated for over a week or so. Nemon and Aramson had therefore devised a way to help conserve their precious commodity. They cut the soap into very small tablets so that as soon as they were done with their bathing and laundry needs, there was barely anything left to hold in one's hand for a decent lather and good scrub.

They swam in the cool water, rinsing off the suds, doing two laps to the far bank and back. Feeling refreshed, they got out and stood on a big rock that jutted into the water and let themselves drip dry as they did not have any bath towels to rub themselves down with.

Nemon told his friend he intended to ask Jenara for her hand in marriage that evening. He'd already advised the elders of his intention and his old man had assured him he would get his full support and would let him have some cattle for dowry payment.

Jenara was the youngest daughter of a deceased couple. Her parents had died when she was only three years old after a mysterious disease had swept through the village. Some of the survivors of that epidemic remained marked and disabled for life.

She had been taken in and brought up by her aunt who happened to be married to the village medicine man. It was the same medicine man that had supposedly apprehended this woman as she made her way from the grave as he had gone out early to find some medicinal plants.

Jenara's aunt did not have any children of her own so she was happy to have Jenara and treated her like her very own. Nemon was quite certain that if he were to get any accurate details of the incident invoking so much talk and speculation, his sweetheart would probably have first hand information.

Having dried up, they tied their loin clothes back on, picked up their axes and said bye to their friends and headed back to the village for their morning chores of milking the cows and delivering the milk to the houses of the white missionaries at the mission station.

1

Present day Malawi is divided into three regions, North, South and Central. The South and Central regions are mostly populated by the Nyanja (Chewa) speaking people whose ancestors are rumoured to have originated from the Katanga region of the Congo (Zaire). In the south east, as you go toward the Shire Valley you find the *Yao* people and, as you journey up north to the Northern region, you begin to encounter the Tumbuka people, at one time reputed prosperous traders matching their bartering skills with those of the Swahili merchants from the east coast and the tribes of neighbouring Tanzania. To the very north you will find the Nkhonde people and, as you travel south along the shores of Lake Malawi toward Nkhata Bay, you meet the Tonga whose language is similar to *chiTumbuka*. These are but a few tribes that inhabit this tiny landlocked country in Central Africa.

In the 1820s, events taking place way down in the south of the African continent in the Zulu kingdom had a ripple effect and subsequently played a profound and significant role in shaping the lives of the central African people. A number of Zulu chiefs, disenchanted by the authoritarian rule of king *Chaka,* rebelled against him and fled northwards to establish kingdoms of their own. Among these disgruntled chiefs was *Mzilikazi,* who set up his Ndebele kingdom about one hundred miles west of where Pretoria stands today.

Other militant bands led by *Sotshangane, Zwangendaba* and *Nxaba* followed suit and set out to establish states of their own. Of particular interest was the marauding band of Zwangendaba's *impi* (army) which ravaged Swaziland and the lower Limpopo valley, taking with them many captives as they slowly advanced northwards across the Limpopo River. Zwangendaba and his army eventually crossed the Zambezi River in 1835 and proceeded to an area west of Lake Malawi, near Mzimba, where they decided to settle down.

The Chewa people in the south had already seen this *'invincible war machine'* at work. Now it was the turn of the Tumbuka and Tonga to experience the terror and misery that these strange people brought along with them. For ten years, Zwangendaba and his warriors terrorized the peaceful people of this region, displacing them from their homes, bringing mayhem and chaos wherever they trod.

These people were addicted to war and killing. Fighting had always been their way of life and, in an ambitious move, Zwangendaba set off to raid areas further up north, eventually reaching the southern end of *Lake Tanganyika* where he fell ill and died in about 1845.

His death caused a rift amongst these Nguni people leading to a division of this notorious band into several smaller groups. One group went up further north while another, led by *Mpezeni,* returned south and settled in the area of Fort Jameson. The third group, under Mbelwa, one of Zwangendaba's sons, returned to the same area west of Lake Malawi and settled down near *Eswazini* from where they subjugated the Nkhonde, Tonga and Tumbuka people, subsequently destroying the dynasties of *Chikulamayembe* and *Kasungu.*

In 1879, the Tumbuka people rebelled and chief Mbelwa let loose his army. They spared no one, massacring all survivors that had taken refuge on *Hora* Mountain near present day *Lunjika* and *Mbelwa Farm Institute.*

Mbelwa, now paramount chief, appointed his brothers *Mpherembe* and *Mthwalo* as chiefs to help him govern his ever expanding territory. Chief Mawulawo was to govern in the southern part of the territory and up north, towards *Emchinseni,* he sent his brother Mpherembe and further up north toward *Edundu,* his other brother Mthwalo set up shop. This Jere clan was to the local people what the Khumalos were to the Ndebele people.

Most of their villages bore Zulu names. Places like *Efelanja, Ekwaliweni, Emazinyeni, Engcongolweni* and *Ekwendeni,* just to mention a few. As society expanded and more villages were established, people mixed and intermarried and, as a result, the two languages of Zulu and Tumbuka began to be spoken by the whole community. However, Zulu culture and tradition was the cornerstone of this society. Therefore, during certain ceremonies, the people of Ekwendeni were required to don their traditional Zulu apparel. This day, when a special court session had been called for by the chief, was one such day when Zulu lore and culture would be observed to the hilt.

2

The kraal was almost bursting at the seams with people, everyone so keenly interested to witness the proceedings of this extraordinary case. It looked like they had been drawn by a magnet or like flies to a dead animal. Some people had come in from as far as Kasito, every one of them having put aside their normal duties just to be there to witness for themselves.

Anything to do with sorcery was a serious crime in this society. It always had been so in the Zulu tradition. Therefore, it was no surprise that here in Ekwendeni, where Lithini Jere was now chief, Zulu was still the official court language and Zulu law still reigned supreme.

The shout of *'Bayethe'* from the direction of the chief's house and the ensuing clapping of hands by the women and their ululating signaled the approach of the chief. A stool had been placed at the top of the mound in the center of this big *indaba kraal*. As the chief, clad in leopard skin from head to feet, walked through the entrance, followed by high-ranking members of his judicial council, the *ingoma* dancers broke into a warrior dance and song. The dancers were all clad in monkey skin kilts and each carried a body length shield in one hand and a short *assegai* spear in the other.

One of the warriors, in his husky but far reaching voice, led the group in a song, the rest joining in with their mellow baritone and high-pitched voices, jumping into the air in unison and gyrating in perfect harmony, their movements one fluid motion, throwing up their arms in a synchronized movement and letting the toughened brown and white ox-hide shields catch the noon's glare of the sun.

They made mock stabbing gestures with their spears, catapulting themselves back from their imaginary foe. They lifted their feet high up in the air and brought them down in a timed solid rhythmic stomping of the ground that raised dust from the hard packed earth. These were the elite dancers, the very best. It had taken them many painful years to master this unique dance.

The women, on the one side, accompanied the men's singing with their shrill voices, swaying their bare-breasted bodies to this beautiful music.

Forming two lines from the entrance of the kraal, they sang praises to the chief as he walked in between them toward his stool at the center of the kraal. As he reached his seat, with his counselors, six on each side of him, standing just in front of him a few feet below, he rose up his *assegai* spear in his right hand and bellowed out what sounded like a greeting.

'*Bayethe nkosi,* Hail the chief' the crowd responded.

He stood for a moment, surveying his subjects and, after a short while, sat down, his advisors doing likewise. From now on, everyone would be required to keep quiet except for those people specifically requested to give testimony by the court's spokesperson.

The only sound one could hear was the drone of the big green flies as they made their way from one sweaty body to another, quickly evading a swat here and there.

As tradition required, the women sat on the one side and the men on the other.

After some short deliberation with his counsel, the chief indicated he was ready for the proceedings to begin.

The spokesperson immediately launched himself into a chant which was picked up by the *ingoma* dancers and the crowd. He sang praises to the almighty *Nkulunkulu,* the omnipotent God, and thanked Him for the good leadership that the people experienced. He asked that wisdom be bestowed on the counsel gathered there on that day and for common sense and justice to prevail as they discussed an *indaba* of great concern.

He went on and on for what seemed to be an eternity until the air was filled with dust from the stomping feet of the dancers.

'*Bayethe baba nkosi*', he shouted as he brandished his spear. The crowd responded in the same manner amid a cacophony of coughing and sneezing, people pinching their noses and blowing hard to get rid of the trapped dirt in their nostrils, wiping off the mucus on their hands against their thighs.

Some people coughed and cleared their throats aiming their sputum expertly at some opening in the ground, quickly covering it with some thin film of dust with the aid of their feet.

Signaling the dancers to stop, the spokesperson turned to the chief and began to explain the purpose of this gathering. He went on to narrate how the news had been received that morning about an incident that had taken place in Emazinyeni village. For a more detailed account, he said he would now call upon the medicine man that had apprehended the accused woman.

'*Mayibuye inyanga*'

'Let the medicine man approach' he shouted.

From outside the kraal came an eerie cry and, in a staccato like motion, the medicine man made his way toward the group of elders in the center of the kraal.

Around his neck hung a necklace of small bird bones and crocodile teeth, some red and black beads and the treated skin of a python snake.

His head gear consisted of eagle and owl feathers and on his forehead hung a small monkey skull. In his right hand he carried a long fly whisk which he continuously dipped into a greasy black gourd in his left hand and swished the mixture in all directions as he made his way to the center of the kraal.

Nemon, seated near the entrance of the kraal, felt a chill run down his spine when he recognized Jenara's uncle. He wondered how they would get along.

On the medicine man's back was a crocodile skin bag that seemed to contain something heavy. As he neared the mound, he fell down on his knees and asked for permission to proceed with his testimony.

'*Baba nkosi*, Honorable Chief,' he began in a sharp voice that carried far and wide. He went on to explain how he had been woken up from his deep sleep in the middle of the night by some spirit telling him to go to a certain hill where he would find a particular herb, and on his way from that hill, he had heard some strange noises from the direction of the village cemetery.

When he went to check on the noise, he found the accused woman, *Ma Nyoni*, about to hightail it from the graveyard. He then noticed that one grave seemed to have been tampered with and the soil looked freshly dug.

Summoning his spirits, he'd then cast a spell on the woman instantly immobilizing her movements. The accused woman had been stark naked and had a big bag slung over her shoulder. In any other circumstance, he would have driven a stake through her head, killing her instantly. But, he had reasoned that, as there seemed to be an increased activity of witch-craft in the villages, this perpetrator better be brought to court and whatever sentence was given to her, could perhaps serve as a deterrent to all other witches.

From the big bag, he brought out what seemed to be a decomposing head of a small child, a similarly decomposed leg and what looked like some male genitalia. He laid everything down on the ground. This, he said, was what he had recovered from the woman's bag.

He had then alerted the village headman who had in turn made arrangements for the accused woman to be dispatched to the chief's kraal.

'This is all your servant has to say, my lord,' the medicine man concluded as he bowed his head in respect.

'*Ngiyabonga*. Thank you,' the chief replied and gestured for the witness to leave the 'stand '.

He turned to his counsel and asked them what they thought about the matter now in their hands. They deliberated in low tones, only the nodding of their heads indicating that whatever it was that they were discussing, they were in unanimous agreement.

Having finally come to a consensus, the chief asked the spokesperson to have the accused woman brought in. The woman had been brought in from Emazinyeni in an ox-drawn cart covered with a tarpaulin and been bundled into a small hut upon arrival. The door had been latched tight from outside and a group of athletic looking young men stood guard around the windowless hut.

At the signal, the door was opened and the poor woman dragged out into the bright sunlight which momentarily blinded her. She was hauled unceremoniously into the kraal while she screamed and made some incongruous noises through her mouth.

The crowd began to shout.

"*Mthakathi, makabulawe*. Witch, let her be killed, " they chanted.

With her hands still tied behind her back, the two young men dragged her and dropped her in front of the chief and his counsel and hastily retreated.

"*Ngixolele nkosi, bekungasintando yami baba.*"

"Forgive me my lord, this was not of my own doing," the woman shrieked and sprawled down on her stomach and repeatedly struck her forehead to the ground. The chief raised his spear into the air and silence fell over the overcrowded kraal.

He cleared his throat and asked the woman if she knew what she was being accused of and if she recognized all the material lying before her. The woman explained that there was a possibility she had been possessed by some evil spirit which had made her do what she had done and asked for pardon as this was not entirely her fault.

"You realize that witchcraft is not allowed in our society," the chief said to her, "yet you went out and desecrated a burying ground in total disregard of our traditional laws and you expect me to believe that you did not know what you were doing?" the chief asked her in an unbelieving tone.

"This is outrageous and unrighteous," he continued. "After much deliberation, it is this court's decision that, owing to the severity of this matter, you be put to death in the manner that witches have for a long time been executed in our tradition," the chief said with a stern look on his face.

"You will, therefore, when the sun goes down, be axed to death by the only person empowered to do so, the medicine man," he concluded.

Turning around to face the crowd, he raised his voice and addressed the crowd and warned them that as long as he remained chief, he would see to it that witchcraft was eradicated from his villages.

"I therefore declare this court session over," he ended his speech.

The accused woman screamed obscenities and, with froth running from her mouth as if possessed, her voice suddenly changing into a deep male voice, she turned to the medicine man who was crouching at a distance away from the proceedings and started to curse him.

"You are cursed, medicine man," the voice said, "I will come to devour your children and grand children and they will die the same death as mine, be warned."

The possessed woman wriggled like a serpent on the ground while the same young men picked her up and towed her back into the small hut.

The chief stood up and, followed by his advisors, left the kraal as the *ingoma* dancers once again broke into song and dance.

Nemon tugged his friend Aramson, "Let's get out of here before the stampede begins," he said as he quickly made his way towards the single exit.

When the sun went down, the medicine man, assisted by his two apprentices, would systematically proceed to put the woman to death.

With hand and legs pegged to the ground, using thin, long, sharp and needle pointed spatula like iron instruments, they would carefully and slowly plunge these into the eye sockets, work them around the cavities and pop out the eyes one at a time.

Amidst the incessant screaming, they would go on to chop her clean shaven head, chipping off her skull one small piece at a time using very small axes, removing the brain in the process and storing it in a gourd. They would then dismember the body and burn the various human parts in a bonfire that could be seen from many miles away.

All this was performed at the top of the hill known as *Chinungu*. Only the witchdoctors were allowed to go up this hill. As usual, this incident would invoke a sharp outcry from the white missionaries at the Livingstonia Mission Station.

3

Leaving the events of the day behind him, Nemon set out to finish his afternoon chores before finally fishing out his Sunday best clothes. He pulled down some crumpled knee length khaki pants hanging from a string that ran across the room. He also plucked down a khaki shirt that was missing three buttons and showed advanced signs of wear and tear. His short was held up around his waist with the aid of a strip of bark twine. He did not own any shoes at all. His heels bore a myriad of deep cracks witch defied even the extra heavy scrubbing with a very rough piece of stone they were often subjected to.

His friends taunted him all the time saying those cracks were deep enough to hide a tickey coin.

He fastened his shirt using two big safety pins that he normally used to pry out some stubborn thorns from under his feet. After surveying himself, he declared himself presentable enough to make a dignified appearance before his girlfriend.

Nemon hoped his friend Aramson would not be late today like he had been the last time they had gone visiting. As if reading his friend's mind, Aramson hailed him from outside his small hut, the *mphara*.

It was custom that, when boys and girls reached puberty, they moved out of their parents' houses and built themselves small huts where they could socialize easily with their friends without causing inconvenience to the elders.

The boys' huts were called *mphara* and the girls', *nthanganeni*. This arrangement also enabled the young people to court and discuss issues with a certain degree of freedom but always under the surveillance of the elders. All suitors were supposed to be announced to the elders as soon as they arrived for a visit.

The structure of these huts consisted of wooden poles dug firmly into the ground and mud used to plaster both the inside and the outside. Intricate designs in various forms and shapes and in a variety of colours were emblazoned on the outside walls. Normally this handwork was done by the very industrious and innovative womenfolk of the village, especially the young girls.

Aramson was dressed in a sky blue shirt with only a couple of buttons on it. His red short had been hacked off at the knees with a not-so-sharp knife, giving them that forlorn appearance. The entire area of his behind was covered with a green hand sewn patch and, like Nemon, his pants were belted around his waist by a strip of leather thong.

Around his neck was a yellow tie with thin brown stripes. Nemon marveled at the way his friend looked. He surely wanted to draw some girl's attention. They complemented each other on their looks and after completing some other rudimentary duties, Nemon advised his friend it was time to hit the road.

They walked through the village, drawing stares from envious younger boys and guffaws and giggles from the village girls who just did not understand why the young men of the village preferred to go elsewhere in search of a bride, more often than not, choosing some ugly girls from some unknown village.

Nemon and Aramson walked along the small path lined with syringa and jacaranda trees on either side, past one family's burial lot and on toward the Moyos' and the Luhangas' homesteads, steadily making their way to the Lunyangwa river about five miles away.

The Lunyangwa was a treacherous river, flowing gently at one moment and, suddenly turning into a raging torrent, swelling from bank to bank as several streams from upland in Mzuzu and the Viphya Mountains poured their waters into it.

On reaching the bank, they stripped off, waded into the water and made their way across the river with their clothes held up high over their heads as the water reached just below their armpits.

On the far bank, they laid down their clothes on the rocks and took a final rinse in the cool waters, combed out their hair, and waited in the late afternoon sunlight to dry off.

Nemon recalled how his uncle had come home one day and told him of this girl any parent would be proud to have as a daughter-in-law. This girl, his uncle had said, was from Emazinyeni village.

She was supposedly fair and good looking, hard working and of good character. Above all, she was a girl who had much respect for the elderly. These were the main traits which most people sought in a woman. So Nemon had taken it upon himself to go calling and verify this information. He had not been disappointed at all.

Jenara was slim, dark in complexion and of an average build. She had long braided hair that hung back to the nape of her neck. She walked with a sensuous swing of her hips and the well-formed muscles in her legs and arms were evidence enough of the hard worker she was.

Having dried up, they put on their clothes and continued on their four-mile final walk through the forest and the gullies, reaching Jenara's village as the red sun took its final bow in the western horizon.

They made straight for Jenara's *nthanganeni* and announced themselves. A small boy ran to the cooking hut where Jenara was and advised her she had visitors. She came out of the hut and approached Nemon and his friend. After exchanging some greetings, she led them into her *nthanganeni*.

She laid out a reed mat for them and after more pleasantries had been exchanged, she offered them a gourd of fresh sweet fermented beer known as *mahewu*. She left them sipping this nutritious brew while she went out and got a few of her friends to come and help her entertain her visitors.

Tradition did not allow that she be alone with her boyfriend at any time before they were married. A big rooster was slaughtered and supper prepared for the prospective son-in-law, the *umkhwenyana*.

They talked well into the night with Aramson paying special attention to one fair skinned girl who was well endowed with big breasts and a sizeable behind. They discussed the events of the day in hushed tones and as it was night, they agreed not to dwell too much on the subject lest the dead woman's wandering spirit hear and punish them.

Having exhausted all topics possible, Nemon finally broke the news to Jenara and asked her the big question.

"I have known you for quite some time now and have fallen in love with you deeply. Will you do me the honor and marry me?" Nemon popped the question.

Jenara just could not contain herself. She asked to be excused and flew out of the hut to go inform the aunt of this good news.

Later on they made arrangements as when to have emissaries sent over to come and ask Jenara's family for the 'flame' *(moto)*, and negotiate the dowry price.

With the dates agreed upon and after making sure that justice had been done to the chicken meat, they finally retired in the early hours of the morning. Nemon and Aramson slept on the one side of the room while the four girls slept on the other side. Nemon contemplated the events of the day and reckoned that things were shaping up as he had planned.

In his fuzzy mind, he began to design his house in which he would live with his wife and family. He made a mental note to ask his friend and the other guys to assist him cut down poles for the house so they could start putting up the structure within the next few weeks.

When he finally fell asleep, he had already decided on how the house would look like. He drifted off into dreamland, dreaming of his wedding and a bevy of children, his children.

4

After the death of David Livingstone in 1874, the Free Church of Scotland agreed to set up a mission in Malawi in memory of the deceased explorer. It was decided that the mission would be called Livingstonia Mission. Amongst the group of people sent out to embark on this project was Dr. Robert Laws of the United Presbyterian Church.

In 1881, the first mission station was set up amongst the Tonga people at Bandawe and this incident infuriated Chief Mbelwa. Chief Mbelwa had wanted the white missionaries to settle within his immediate territory and be within easy reach for him.

Hence, to show his anger at this rebuttal by the white settlers, he unleashed his army on the Tonga people who were living around the mission station, forcing them to flee and live afloat in their boats on the lake. Some people took refuge on the islands in the middle of the lake.

This incursion disrupted the missionaries' activities and, as a result, Dr. Laws set out to speak to the chief about the possibility of stopping these barbaric slayings and gaining permission to set up schools and preach Christianity in the chief's territory. Dr. Laws made two visits in 1876 and 1881 in an effort to try and persuade the chief to live peaceably with his neighbours. With the assistance of William Koyi, a South African Zulu missionary, Dr. Laws gained influence over the chief and around 1885, the first mission station was established at Njuyu.

In 1889, Dr. Elmslie set up another mission station at Ekwendeni under chief Mthwalo's jurisdiction.

In 1894, the mission headquarters, for some reason, were moved from Bandawe to Livingstonia (Khondowe) and soon this center became an oasis of knowledge for not only Nyasaland (Malawi), but for the whole region.

Evangelists, teachers, skilled craftsmen and many more were trained at this institution and, after qualifying, they went out to staff the many schools and churches that were sprouting up throughout the area.

Ekwendeni was one place that benefited from the training of the locals here at Khondowe. Under the supervision of the missionaries, these trained bricklayers and masons built a church of such exquisite beauty never before seen in this part of the country. The architectural structure of this building was beyond description. It was a sight from medieval England, as if magically plucked up from the meadowlands of countryside Coventry and planted here, lost in this tropical thick-forested wild African interior.

It was in this beautiful church at Ekwendeni Mission Station that Nemon, a born again Christian, was joined in holy matrimony to his sweetheart Jenara. It was a simple ceremony attended by about a hundred relatives of both bride and groom.

The day was spent in celebration as people ate and drank while they showered the newly weds with various gifts.

The master of ceremonies, a man selected for his outstanding humorous repertoire, entertained the crowd with his never-ending antics and wisecrack jokes.

The people came to him and described to him what they knew about the bride and groom, in the long run announcing what gift it is that they brought for the newly wed couple.

This went on and on until sundown when a dance was held in a hastily built corral. Here, the young men and women got a chance to intermingle and, on many occasions, log term relationships were founded from such meetings.

Late that evening, after the *zowala* (wedding), Nemon and Jenara, seated in their sleeping chambers in the company of some elderly women, were given a lecture on the basic principles of married life. These women went over every small detail regarding the do's and don'ts and what duties were expected of each person to the other.

After the long torturous lecture, the newly weds were finally left alone to explore their marital bliss and, for the first time in their relationship, they got into each other's arms and, in the faint glow of candle light, their passions running high, they sailed away into uncharted waters.

5

Two months after they were married, Jenara fell pregnant and immediately sought out Nemon's aunt to let her know she had not 'been to the moon', so to say. Aunt Zinzile advised her on how to take care of herself and how important it was not to do too many strenuous chores during this time when a new life was forming within her.

It was a time to rejoice within the Gumbo clan once news leaked out that their daughter in law was with child. At least, they were assured that their malokazana (daughter in law) was capable of helping keep the clan name alive and they all hoped it would be a boy.

Jenara gave birth to a bouncy baby girl and Nemon's father named her Siphiwe, meaning a gift from God. The new parents were ecstatic and, devout Christians that they were, as soon as Siphiwe turned two months, they brought her before the congregation and had Reverend Ziba baptize her.

Siphiwe grew up under the loving care of both her parents and grandparents. She was adored.

It was a family that God blessed richly over the period.

Each year, Nemon and Jenara had a good harvest of maize and other crops. They stored whatever they needed and sold the rest to the traders at Ekwendeni market. Their small herd of cattle and goats also began to grow. The first two years they were together were just blissful, almost too good to be true. It was as if they lived right beneath the shadow of God's hand.

Their fortune changed, however, when Jenara fell pregnant again. From the very onset of her pregnancy, she complained of incessant headaches and stomach pains.

She spent most of the time at the outpatient department and at the antenatal clinic at the hospital.

One morning, as she got out of her house to go fetch some drinking water from the river, about fifteen yards down the path from the house, she stepped on some human excreta.

In the faint light of dawn she had not noticed the small pile of faeces and her bare foot had landed squarely on the matter. She quickly wiped away the sticky smelly mess from under her foot by rubbing it off on the dusty ground, moving her foot vigorously to and fro until there was very little trace of it left.

She picked up a piece of stick and tried to poke away some of the stuff that had gotten stuck in between her toes, all the time cussing herself for not having noticed the mound in her hurry to get to the river.

As she bent down to pick up another piece of stick, she noticed a soiled black oily piece of cloth adorned with human hair and placed right round the human waste. Some red and black seeds lay around the fresh pile, and what seemed to be drops of blood spotted the surrounding area.

Now, this really brought some concern to her and, instead of proceeding to the river, she went back to the house and woke up her husband. With sleep still in his eyes, Nemon followed his wife out and examined this spectacle, cautiously probing the clothing with a long stick.

Someone was sick in his head, Nemon thought as he skirted the mass, making sure he did not get within the circle of blood.

Now, why would anyone take some time to do this kind of foolish thing within the perimeters of his home, he pondered. He weighed the situation and concluded that the elders would better handle this matter.

He went and woke up his father and aunt and they all gathered around and subjected the material to full scrutiny. They all agreed that someone was either trying to play a prank or had some evil intentions and meant harm to this family. Aunt Zinzile took it upon herself to clear the mess, raking it onto a piece of rusty iron sheet and depositing the contents into the pit latrine.

Despite being a Christian family, these folk were very superstitious. So, they agreed to ask the medicine man to come cleanse the house in case of any evil intent on the household following this absurd and ridiculous incident.

Maybe the ordeal played a psychological effect on Jenara or, maybe, what followed was a direct result from her contact with the smelly mass she had stepped on. Whatever it was, her health became a cause for concern. She developed a fever one night and started screaming and hallucinating, claiming she saw a naked woman with talon like finger-nails, floating in the air and giving chase to her daughter Siphiwe.

And, just before the woman in her dream would reach out and snatch her child away, Jenara would wake up, still struggling with this invisible person and drenched in heavy sweat. Nemon would hold her tight in his arms and comfort her, all the while telling her it was just a dream.

When the medicine man did come to perform the cleansing of the houses, he went into a deep trance and announced that he detected the presence of an evil female spirit. A black fowl was killed, the blood left to drip into a gourd and the meat cooked in an earthenware pot that contained a number of medicinal roots, giving the meat some bitter taste.

Everyone in the family was asked to partake of this meat so as to ward off this evil spirit. Some more medicine was planted outside around the houses, and the inside walls were splattered with medicine mixed with the fowl's blood.

For a little while thereafter, Jenara seemed to get better and went back to her normal routine.

One night, into her seventh month of pregnancy, she suddenly developed stomach cramps and began to moan and writhe in pain, prompting Nemon to wake up and summon the assistance of his mother and aunt.

There followed a torturous four hours as the number of elderly women from the village began to grow, all coming to attend to his wife.

Nemon sat huddled in his mother's cooking hut having blown the fire back into life and added a few logs to keep himself warm. For Jenara, it was an experience like she'd never known existed before. Never in her young life had she experienced such excruciating pain. The pain seemed to creep from the pelvic area and ascended slowly up her tummy. As it reached the belly button area, it mushroomed into some sort of explosion, a searing pain that seemed to tear her insides and left her screaming in an uncontrollable frenzy. As the pain grew in intensity and rolled in wave after wave, she finally succumbed thankfully into the dark of unconsciousness.

She was revived by the gentle splash of cold water to her face, only to discover that she had begun some vaginal discharge. Blood mixed with the birth water oozed out like from a steady stream. It was at this time that the attending midwives decided there was nothing more they could possibly do to help her, except get her to the hospital as soon as possible and let the white sisters perform their miracle on her.

Nemon hastily hitched up two oxen to his cart and bundled a number of empty sacks on to the floor so as to make a decent cushion for his wife. Jenara, with the aide of the elderly women, was helped onto the cart and made to lie down as Nemon frantically urged the oxen into a gentle run.

Aunt Zinzile with three other women kept on attending to Jenara in the cart, all the while urging her to hold on and be strong. About a mile away from the hospital, Jenara delivered a stillborn baby boy.

The women wrapped the baby in soft calico clothing and when they reached the hospital, handed the bundle over to the nursing sisters. Jenara was admitted immediately and a blood transfusion performed, perhaps just saving her from the clutches of death.

Nemon leaned against the Post Natal Ward wall and let his tears roll down his face, saddened at the loss of his child. He lifted his eyes into the sky and cried out to his God in helplessness.

"Please God, help me be strong and, thank you for saving my wife." He concluded his prayer.

The baby was buried the following day at the hospital cemetery in a small grave with no markings.

6

After her discharge from hospital, Jenara was allowed to return to her home village of Emazinyeni to recuperate and undergo some traditional ritual to help her get better.

Her young husband was devastated to say the least. His wife had been so close to death, it felt unreal. Despite his Christian belief, his other side still strongly suspected his wife's misfortune might have been the work of some evil entity. So, struggling against his conscience, he made that call on the medicine man and asked him to come cleanse his home again.

Nemon had been to visit his wife the day before and had been pleased to see how well his wife looked. Her health had improved considerably and he had asked her to stay for as long as she wanted till she regained her full strength.

For him, it was a period of deep reflection. What had gone wrong? Had he perhaps done something bad that had, maybe, angered his God or some ancestral spirit?

The more he tried to find a logical explanation to the recent happenings, the more he drew a blank.

Often, his friend Aramson would visit and keep him company, taking him away from his troubled thoughts. One day as they sat by the fire grilling some maize cobs, Nemon confided in his friend that he still was worried and did not absolutely make head or tail of what had happened to his wife.

Did he, Aramson, ever remotely recall him say anything bad to anyone who might have been so offended as to try and harm his family.

"You know you have never had any altercation with anyone since I've known you," Aramson said to his friend.

"But," Aramson paused as he gathered his thoughts together and pulled his stool closer to the fire, "I have been thinking real hard myself" he said hesitantly.

"What?" Nemon asked.

Aramson turned to face his friend, his chin in his hand and a small furrow on his brow.

"Go ahead and tell me your thoughts," Nemon cajoled him.

Aramson was a very superstitious person. Taking his time, he reminded his troubled friend of the day they had attended the court hearing where the accused woman had been found guilty of witchcraft and Jenara's uncle had been appointed to perform the ritual of disposing her off.

"Yes, what about it?" Nemon asked.

"Do you remember what her last words were to Jenara's uncle?" Aramson said to his friend.

"You mean to say that what that demented woman said might have something to do with this?" Nemon queried Aramson.

"I have no doubt whatsoever," his friend answered emphatically, "and I am willing to stake my life on it," he concluded.

After some more deliberation, Aramson got up and bade his friend good day and Nemon walked him out of the yard.

He returned to his seat still trying to grasp the meaning of his friend's interpretation of events.

Could it be his friend was right?

It was incredulous that words so carelessly spoken over thirty months ago by some deranged woman would bear such tragic consequences. The more he reran the events of that day in his mind, the more confused he became. Aramson's train of thought at times seemed to make sense.

He just did not know what to believe anymore.

In the end, Nemon determined he was not going to let such a stupid thing drive him crazy. Had not the white missionaries taught him about a loving and caring God that took all his kind of burdens away?

He was a believer and a baptized Christian and he would put everything into the Lord's hands. He believed in the power of prayer and whatever the Almighty gave him, that he would gladly accept.

Such was his unwavering belief in the God of Isaac and Abraham, the God of Israel that so many of his friends found so hard to comprehend. They claimed this was a white man's god who could understand neither their language nor the needs and minds of the black person.

Despite the criticism from relatives and friends, Nemon still got down on his knees and asked for forgiveness of sins and also asked for blessings for his young family.

While Jenara recuperated in her home village, Siphiwe stayed with Nemon's parents. She was a happy go kid and so full of life. Nemon marveled and smiled as this bundle of energy and fun kept everyone full of laughter. As her name implied, she was indeed a gift from God.

Jenara came back home after two months. She had fully recovered and was full of vigour. Her stay in Emazinyeni had really worked wonders on her. She immediately launched herself to the task of tidying up the house which definitely showed signs of female neglect. It was a happy family reunion.

Before long, things went back to normal and soon all the unhappy memories were stored away. With the rains approaching, the villagers began to prepare their fields and Nemon and Jenara did likewise. They buried themselves into their work and cleared a new patch of land for their *rapoko* crop. They cut down the small trees and bushes, gathered them into stacks and set them alight. The burning wood would provide the vital nutrients to the soil that would enable them have a healthy crop, Nemon explained to the ever inquisitive Siphiwe.

As the rainy season drew nearer and nearer each day, so the land preparation activities grew more and more frantic. Faces would look up into the sky and each one would proclaim that the rains would surely come down the next day.

When the rains finally came two weeks later, it was so sudden and unexpected. It had dawned a clear morning with the sun shining bright, clear blue skies with no speck of cloud in sight.

People went out to the fields and tilled the land, making undulating ridges for their maize crop.

Six hours later, heavy clouds began to drift in from the direction of the Viphya Mountains and the day began to darken as the thick *cumuli nimbus* clouds began to blanket the sky.

The rumble of thunder could be heard rolling long and far. Lightning flashed, very vivid and lighting up the dark heavens. Nemon looked up and surmised it was unsafe to continue working in the open fields and announced to his wife it was time to go.

Judging by the way the storm was building up, Nemon reckoned they would not be able to make it to the river in time and suggested that (seeing they were closer to Jenara's village) they go and seek shelter there till the storm passed.

Jenara bundled Siphiwe on her back and they hurriedly left for her aunt's place as big drops began to fall from the sky. They made it in the nick of time.

The whole sky opened up. It was hard pounding rain that caused poorly constructed roofs to sag and drip, others to crumble and fall.

Just like Noah's rain, Nemon soliloquized.

The lightning was incessant and, Siphiwe, not used to such heavenly activity, cowered under her *mbeleko* behind on her mother's back, tucking her head in and refusing to come out till she went to sleep. Not even the offer of food could entice her to come out of her secure position.

It rained for two hours without let and in the end, they decided to spend the night there. About midnight, the rain tapered off to a steady drizzle which continued till just about dawn when it gradually stopped.

The ground was a quagmire. All the little streams were torrentious. The rumble of the Lunyangwa could be heard form afar. It was an ominous and gentle, but frightful roar. The morning air was clean, sharp and very refreshing.

The cattle all struggled to get to the top of the mound in the middle of the kraal where it was less muddy than at the base.

This was not rain that brought life and sustenance to the people and their crops. This was wrecking rain, rain that brought with it havoc, mayhem and damage to vegetation and human life. No work could done in the fields after such a downpour. Nemon and Jenara decided they would head for home as soon as it was decent enough for them to bid farewell.

They used a circuitous route, avoiding the full streams, dongas and gullies, making for the sole bridge that crossed the Lunyangwa River and served as a link between the Mission station and the villages of **Emazinyeni** and **Enyezini**.

It was an unbelievable sight that met their eyes as soon as they walked into their home village.

Where once had stood their lovely house was just charred remains, everything razed to the ground. Lightning bolts had struck the house an incredible three times torching it.

7

Fellow villagers assisted them in putting up a new house. Thatching grass was donated by relatives and friends and, three weeks after their house had been destroyed, Nemon and Jenara moved into their second new house.

Each time the rains came, Nemon would say a silent prayer and ask for protection from the Lord.

The rainy season finally came to an end and after a little while, the crop was ready for gathering.

It was at this time that Jenara told Nemon she was pregnant again. Concerned about her health, aunt Zinzile and Nemon's mother assisted her to gather in her crop.

It was a good harvest. When the Thanks giving Service was conducted, they took the various crops to church as offering *(this is a tradition that has continued to this day)* and thanked the Lord for a good harvest.

Nemon became more and more involved in church activities and was soon appointed Sunday School teacher for the little children. Each Sunday morning, with Siphiwe in tow, he would head for the mission station and there, from eight 'o clock in the morning to nine thirty, he would tell the little ones interesting stories from the Bible. It was a blessing to able to share with these young and innocent ones.

Meanwhile, his wife was doing better than expected. During one of her ante-natal visits to the hospital, after having palpated and listened to her tummy, the nursing sister told her that she probably had a set of twins coming. She was advised to take it easy and get plenty of rest. Her tummy grew very big and made her huff and puff as she struddled around performing her duties.

Upon noticing the difficulty she was experiencing, Nemon asked for someone to assist her with her chores and a young girl was sent in from Jenara's village. Jenara continued to perform some light duties but when she next went in for her check up, she was detained at the hospital.

On the first day when the rains came again, she gave birth to twin boys. There was no complication at all with either the mother or the young ones. The nursing sisters showered her with gifts of baby clothes and other useful things

It was a beaming Nemon that escorted his wife from the hospital the day she was discharged.

He named the boys Khumbulani and Khumbolithu.

He was probably the happiest man in the village, a very proud father. He played with his boys each time he came back from the fields and they developed a very strong bond. Together with Siphiwe, they formed an incredible foursome.

Jenara would often smile in satisfaction as she watched this Gumbo brood go about all kinds of antics that sometimes nearly made her heart skip a beat.

The boys grew fast and at two years, were running about and causing a lot of anxiety. From even such an early age, one could detect the protective tendencies that these little guys extended toward one another. No sooner would one of them be embroiled in some fight with another kid than the other would come to his brother's aid. They were dubbed the *terrible twins*. What mattered most was that they brought joy and laughter to this small family.

One summer afternoon as the sun prepared to descend down to its resting place and the cattle and goats were being herded back into the kraals and pens, the twins wandered off to watch their father's goats being penned in.

A big black he-goat from another pen was going about *tormenting* one of their father's female goats, chasing the goat mercilessly around all over the place. Now, this did not sit well with Khumbulani as he watched this intruder goat continually harass one of *his goats*. Agitated he became and decided he was going to put a stop to this whole nuisance. Picking up a small piece of stick, he began to chase this unwanted goat away.

The goat was not amused. Looking at this small two legged being that tried to interrupt its mating advances, the goat suddenly turned around and, lowering its head crowned with long curving horns, charged at this annoying little person, bashing him straight on the head, smashing Khumbulani's face as he tried in vain to ward off the charge with his small outstretched hands.

Khumbolithu, seeing his brother bawled over, decided to come to the rescue, but the goat was not going to be stopped by these little nincompoops.

The goat turned around and faced this new threat. It lowered its head again and charged at Khumbolithu, again ramming its full horned head into the small face, crushing the little body to the ground.

This happened so fast that by the time the herd boys realized what had happened, the two children lay on the ground, blood gushing from their heads, still and dead. Two lives snatched away in a most bizarre kind of incident.

The village elders could not believe what they heard from the herd boys. No such thing had ever happened before. This was more than a freak accident, they concluded.

The Gumbo family was more than devastated, shattered to say the least. What would it take, Nemon cried, to try and maintain some happiness in this household.

It was like his family had been singled out for punishment by some invisible force.

To say Jenara was stunned would be an understatement. She was hysterical and it took several women to subdue her.

They tried in all ways possible to comfort and soothe her and, well into the night, she began to calm down and pleaded that she at least see her sons one last time.

"Why is this happening to me?" she cried, "what have I done to deserve this horror and misfortune?" she wailed as tears drenched the front of her dress.

Throughout the night, the people from within and without the village gathered to comfort this young family. They sang hymns and quoted scriptures, urging the bereaved couple to be strong and trust in the Lord.

When morning came, the two small bodies, wrapped in some new clothing, were laid to rest beneath the *mkhaya* tree, in the Gumbos' burial lot.

Immediately, the chief ordered that the goat be killed and the carcass burnt.

An almost palpable void was left in Nemon's life. Despite his strength and composure, the telling effect that these deaths had on him was clearly visible.

A plethora of thoughts ran through his mind. Friends and relatives advised him to seek help from the witchdoctors as this was surely an act perpetrated by some evil entity. Nemon resolved he was not going to do so.

Behind his back they said he was a fool and had been brainwashed by the *mzungu's* religion.

If ever this painful event was supposed to make him change his belief in Christ, it only served to strengthen his resolve and faith in Christianity.

These were indeed trying times for him and his family but, for one thing he was glad, his wife shared in his faith. Together they spent long hours in prayer and comforted each other. They still had Siphiwe and for this they rejoiced.

8

In the winter of 1933, eight years after they had been married, Jenara again conceived and gave birth to a baby girl whom they named *Thandekile* (The loved one).

This time, without Nemon's knowledge and in connivance with their daughter in law, Nemon's parents brought in the medicine man who attended to the baby and gave it medicine to make it strong so that any evil spirits would be warded off.

Amidst the fragrant smoke that he caused by burning certain dried roots on a sheet of zinc, he lifted the baby up and, moving it in a circular motion above the light smoke, the medicine man called upon the good spirits to protect the innocent child from evil and harm. The baby was then bathed in lukewarm water that contained a flotilla of green herbs. Lastly, a thin strip of black cloth with a small bulge of medicine in the middle, was tied around its waist. The ceremony over, the medicine man departed with an assurance that no harm would ever befall the baby.

Siphiwe was overjoyed at having a baby sister at last. She was in constant trail of her mother wherever she went, always asking that the baby be strapped to her back so she could play with it.

With caution, Jenara would carefully and securely strap the baby to Siphiwe's back and keep a close eye on her movements. She became very protective and never allowed her children out of sight unless they were in the company of one of the elders.

Thandi, as *Thandekile* came to be known, was quite a healthy baby. She could suck her mother dry, literally, and still wail for some more.

During one of her monthly visits to the baby clinic at the CCAP hospital, the nursing sisters gave her a feeding bottle and some powdered milk for supplementary feeding. She was also shown how to prepare the milk and how to clean the bottle each time after use.

Thandi took to the bottle like a fish to water. At eight months she was bigger than most babies her age. She was quite a handful and demanded attention all the time.

On one occasion, Jenara being busy with some of her duties and baby Thandi crying to be fed, Siphiwe insisted the she bottle feed her young sister. Jenara sat her down on the doorway of their house and placed the baby on Siphiwe's lap, putting the bottle to the already open mouth of baby Thandi.

Jenara went back to her chores, casting peremptory glances toward her kids to make sure everything was okay.

It seemed only like a moment when she turned away to throw out some dirty washing water before she heard Siphiwe's call for help. She dropped the pot in her hands and rushed to the doorway. The baby was choking and Siphiwe had removed the bottle from its mouth.

Jenara grabbed her baby and slapped it gently on the back of its chest. Nothing.

The baby kept on gasping for air.

She slapped the baby on its back again and again with no better result and began to scream for her mother in law. She upended the baby and tapped it on the back of the chest again and again, all the time urging it to breathe.

Her mother in-law rushed to the scene and took Thandi away from Jenara. She tried her best to let the air into the baby's lungs.

Despite all their frantic efforts, they could not get young Thandi to breathe again and they saw the baby's face begin to turn pale.

Right there, before their very eyes, they watched the life of the precious baby slip away.

Nemon's mother clutched the limp little warm body to her chest and wept, crying out to the gods of her forefathers, asking for an explanation.

"Why... why do you torment me like this?" she lamented, "why don't you just take me and leave my grandchildren alone?" she wept.

The women from the other houses nearby, on hearing this wailing and commotion, rushed to see what was happening. They led the two women into the house, taking the dead baby away and wrapping it in a small blanket, laying it down on a mat.

Soon the news was all over that Jenara had lost her youngest child. Word was sent to Nemon who had gone to the mission station for a church elders' meeting. That night he wept.

Deep wrecking sobs, tears gushing from an interior reservoir that was full of too many unshed tears. It seemed this death triggered off something in him and the pain became so intense, so overwhelming it made him numb all over.

It was an emotional pain he had never before experienced. Men were not supposed to cry openly or show any sign of pain in this society. This time he could not contain himself and the other people seemed to understand.

They let him cry, let him shed his tears of pain, the pain they also felt.

The following day, one more grave was added to the family burying lot beneath the *mkhaya* tree.

After the burial, Nemon met with his father. Sitting down in the awning of the old man's house, they discussed in hushed tones the events that had taken place since Nemon had married Jenara. They both agreed that it did look like their family was being dogged by some eerie misfortune.

In the end, they agreed to do one logical thing.

They would relocate to a place far away from here where, hopefully, these misfortunes would not follow them.

They decided they would go and live in Eswazini where Nemon's aunt, Balekile Gumbo, was married to Chief Kampingo Sibanda. That evening, gathered by the fireside with all their women folk, they advised them what course of action they had decided to take and that every one be prepared for moving. The following day they went to see the chief and advised him of their intentions and he gave them his blessings.

So, two weeks later, with all their belongings gathered together, they rounded up their livestock and set off for Eswazini. It took them four days to get to Kampingo Sibanda's village and Nemon's aunt and the chief were there waiting for them.

9

The Kasito valley nestles in the center of high peaked mountains in what could be a crater formed from long dormant volcanic activity. To the east is the Lunjika range of mountains that protects the valley from the chilly winds blowing from the Viphya plateau and Chikangawa forest. To the west is another range of mountains that encompasses Hora mountain, stretching all the way from Eswazini to Euthini. In the middle of this lush green valley, the Kasito river flows all year long on its journey toward Rumphi.

The Gumbo family was given a tract of land at the base of Lunjika mountain. Pools of icy clear water could be found on the mountain top and these natural reservoirs acted as emergency supplies for both man and wildlife in times of drought. The river was only a stone throw away from the home that they set up.

Nemon and Jenara immediately established a vegetable garden by the banks of the river. Some of the villagers planted sugar cane which seemed to thrive in the marshy conditions there.

With the help of the Sibandas, they soon settled down to a routine village life.

The first year went by without incident and their first crop was good. Their livestock too increased in number and their daughter grew up rapidly with tell-tale signs of budding breasts becoming more visible.

Looking at their daughter, Nemon and Jenara cast aside their fears and apprehensions and decided to have another baby. After several attempts, Jenara finally conceived and gave birth to another set of twins, a boy and a girl. They named the boy Themba and the girl Sithembile.

Their nearest neighbours, the Tomokas, kindly offered them assistance with field duties during this time that Jenara was unable to attend to her crops. Everyone else pitched in to give some help one way or the other.

In the mornings, the village children would wake up early and go stand guard over the maize crop before the troops of baboons descended from the lofty tops of Lunjika mountain to wreak havoc to the corn crop.

It was more difficult, particularly for the women, to stand guard alone because, as soon as the crafty baboons realized there was no male member present, they became more daring and went on ahead to plunder the crop, making token ret reats only when the women got too near them, often making obscene gestures at them.

Not even the presence of dogs would deter these *'people like'* animals once they set up their minds on having a meal. Once, when one fearless dog dared getting too near one big male baboon, it was torn to pieces by the strong troop leader.

April came and with it the Easter holidays. As usual, beginning on a Friday, there was a three day commemoration service of the death and resurrection of Christ.

Nemon, being one of the elected presenters of the Gospel during this long weekend of prayer, left home on a Thursday morning bound for Njuyu mission station where services were to be centered this particular weekend.

He wished his family a happy Easter weekend and, slinging his small *katundu* containing his change of clothing and some cooked food, he set off on the day long walk to the mission station that had been set up by Dr. Elmslie so many years ago and was also the home of Reverend Mawelela Tembo, one of the first Nguni converts and preachers.

(One of Reverend Mawelela's grandsons eventually married one of Nemon's daughters).

It seemed that most of the mishaps and tragic events happened during Nemon's absence and this time was to be no exception. On this Saturday morning, everyone in the village got up early and those that could make it to church for the local service made their way there whilst the others went to tend to the crop.

From the mountains the baboons could be heard barking, getting ready for their assault on the maize fields down below.

As soon as the sun broke over the rugged ridges of the Lunjika mountains, Jenara and Siphiwe, each with a baby strapped to their backs and carrying some provisions for the day, left home to stand guard over their crop. They joined other women folk and children on their way to their fields also, singing worship songs about the Savior that had died for them on the cross.

Maybe it was because no elderly male persons were among this group of watchers on this Saturday morning or, maybe this particular troop of baboons led by two very big males had not had a proper meal in the last few days. Whatever the reason be, on this day, they became menacing and very daring.

When these baboons descended to try their luck, Jenara and Siphiwe, with the help of other women from an adjacent field, managed to drive this troop back up the hill but soon, more baboons came down from another direction into their neighbours' field.

With their friends going off in the other direction, Jenara and Siphiwe were left alone to fend off their group of unwelcome guests. Finding it cumbersome to run to and fro with the babies strapped on their backs, Jenara laid them down under the cool shadows of a big tree.

Each time there was an advance from the baboons, they would get up and chase them away with long sticks flailing in the air and always shouting at the top of their voices.

When the baboons regrouped, they seemed to have '*discussed*' some sort of strategy on how to effectively gain access to the succulent crop because, when they came out the next time, they were in two groups, outflanking Jenara. As soon as she took off after the one group, the other rushed into the field, each baboon quickly grabbing as many cobs as it could carry before hastily retreating a short distance to eat and repeating the same move.

When they came down the third time, Jenara told Siphiwe to chase away the one group while she dealt with the other. When both of them took off in different directions after the baboons, they left the babies unattended.

It was at this moment that the two grand old men of the troop wandered across the babies.

Perhaps, infuriated at being accosted by these women, the one baboon decided to vent its anger on the tiny little ones.

When the second baboon saw the other one grab hold of one baby's foot, it also did likewise.

However, when they saw Jenara running back towards them making some funny noises, they decided they were going to play a game with her.

Tightly clutching the legs of the five month old babies, they took off up the rocky hill, dragging the poor babies behind them, banging their heads on the hard ground of this granite rock hill.

Jenara screamed for help and went after the baboons.

When they finally let go of her babies, they had been dragged across the rocky terrain for about a hundred yards and the small heads were like pulp, their features unrecognizable.

When the other women came to her aid, they found Jenara banging her head on to the rocky ground, wailing incoherently, blood gushing from her head cuts mixing with tears. Some of the women grabbed hold of her in an effort to restrain her while the others picked up the tiny little bodies and started the solemn walk home, leaving the baboons to a free feast.

It was a subdued atmosphere that Nemon returned to on Monday afternoon. His children had been buried the previous day.

When they finally related to him the events that had taken place during his short absence, Nemon was convinced that he would never outrun that invisible hand of death that seemed to stalk his family. With a heavy heart, he went to the small graves to pay his respects to his babies, the first graves in this new home of theirs.

It seemed the earth never quenched its thirst no matter how may bodies it swallowed up, he thought to himself. What use was it that, even if he bore any children, he never reveled in parenthood like the other people did? It was particularly unfair for the woman he loved, the person that carried the unborn babies for nine months and went through the painful periods of labour and delivery.

It was probably better not to have any children.

He sat down and thought deeply and inside his head an idea began to formulate.

10

In the 1800's, most European countries set out to colonize Africa. France, German, Belgium, Holland, Portugal and Great Britain all sent out explorers and settlers to go stake and occupy as much of Africa as they could.

One notable Englishman who was successful at doing this was Cecil John Rhodes. After the British had managed to settle in Mashonaland, setting up Fort Salisbury, and after one nearly disastrous episode, Rhodes wrote to Lord Salisbury, the British Premier then, thus:

"I can not feed the people in Mashonaland by the overland route, and I can not feed them from Beira with ninety miles of fly [tsetse] which kills the oxen. I must have a railroad or a tramway through that piece"

And so, a dream was born. A dream to create an internal 'Suez Canal' , as he put it, by building a railway line from the Cape, through Matebeleland and Fort Salisbury, to Cairo.

In 1897, the railway line from Mafikeng reached Bulawayo and a year later, the line from Beira reached Mashonaland. Little did Cecil Rhodes know what impact this dream of his would have on the natives of most of Central Africa.

When news spread about the jobs being offered by this new railroad company, people flocked in from all directions, from as far north as Tanganyika, to seek some of the fortune that the white man brought with him.

This trend continued through the years into the early 1900's and so it was no surprise that, after the harvest of 1937, Nemon decided he would also journey south to try his luck.

He bade farewell to his family and joined the approximate ten thousand men that left *Nyasaland* each year to go seek work in the more industrially advanced places south of the Zambezi, to Southern Rhodesia and the Union of South Africa, popularly known as Harare and Joni respectively. Journeying with him were four other young men from the same village.

The distance from Emoneni to Mzimba is about forty miles as the crow flies. It took Nemon and his friends the whole day to get there.

The few government trucks that they saw enroute to Mzimba did not stop for them when they flagged them down for a lift instead, left them in a cloud of dust as they sped past them.

When they finally reached Mzimba Boma, it was about four o'clock in the afternoon and the bus to Kasungu and Lilongwe was not scheduled to depart until eight o'clock that same evening.

They stretched out beneath the welcome cool shadow of a big baobab tree eating a little from the food parcels they had brought with them.

Their feet were bathed in brown dust and they made no effort to clean themselves.

Big green flies constantly perched on their sweaty brows and on their food, their reflex actions being not quick enough to dispose of these irritant invaders.

After having eaten conservatively, they got up and slowly trudged off to the water pump to have a drink.

As the sun finally set and the hot sultry air changed to a refreshing cool breeze, energy started to seep back into the tired limbs of these young Nguni men. They discussed their dreams in excited but restrained tones, sometimes painting unrealistic pictures of what they would like to have once they secured jobs in that land of milk and honey.

The bus came and, as always, it was running late. There was a rush to get in line, everyone rushing to get to the bus door and be first in line, shoving and trampling each other, oblivious of the pain they inflicted.

It took the white bus conductor to get the crowd to make one decent line.

Nemon and his pals were amongst the first people at the head of the line and were assured of getting a seat for the eight hour ride to Lilongwe. Some unfortunate travelers, especially those at the very end of the queue, would travel the entire journey standing on their feet.

About one hundred and thirty people were jammed like sardines into this eighty-five seater bus and the heat exuded by the crammed sweaty bodies made it unbearable inside.

With much whistling and singing, the bus started off on its long journey south, following the narrow winding road that was bordered by high trees on both sides.

Occasionally, buck and other wild animals would dart across the road in front of the moving vehicle, forcing the driver to apply the brakes and causing a wave of standing bodies to cannon into the barrier that separated the driver from the passengers.

The bus stopped frequently on the way, putting off a few people that were not proceeding all the way to Lilongwe. When the bus got to Kasungu, there were about twenty standing passengers and the driver announced he was taking a rest for about an hour.

The people were allowed to leave the bus and buy some food from the milling vendors that were still up at this time of the night. Boiled eggs, fried fish, corn bread, bananas and guavas were being sold by the young girls and old women, darting to and fro, screaming out their wares trying to attract as many clients as possible so they could get rid of their day's stock and go catch a few winks of sleep from what few hours were left of the night.

The next day would be a repeat of the same process. If the stock was not sold out on one day, some unwary traveler would purchase it the following day after having been warmed again and spiced a little to cover up the stale taste and smell.

Nemon and his mates got out to stretch their legs and tucked into their small food carriers, eating just enough to quieten their complaining tummies.

Some passengers, presumably those that had been standing for most of the way, stretched out flat on the ground and took a quick nap.

Before long, the driver sounded the horn to indicate it was time to proceed. He was very eager to be on the move and to gain some of that lost time.

With everyone aboard, the second half of the journey began, this time with much fewer stops on the way.

Halfway between Kasungu and Lilongwe, there were no standing passengers any more. Most of the people in the bus were young men, all fuelled by stories of wealth to be had in the gold and diamond mines of *Joni*, all driven by some determination to be a part of this incredible development taking place way down south. When they drove into Lilongwe, the roosters were crowing and dawn was breaking. There was a little chill in the air.

Lilongwe in the early morning hours was reputedly unfriendly both weather wise and people wise.

There was always the danger of frostbite on the one hand and on the other, there were the *kawalalas* (thugs) who preyed on the unsuspecting travelers.

The young men from Emoneni joined a group of other travellers and awaited daylight. As soon as it was light enough and safe to go about, Nemon and his friends started off on foot towards Dedza, hoping to catch a lift on the way.

It took them another two days to get to the small town of Blantyre and by that time, their supplies had run pretty low. Two of Nemon's pals, excited at seeing the city for the first time, decided they were not going any further.

Nemon and the other two guys were lucky to hitch a ride from one road haulier who was going all the way to Tete in Portuguese East Africa and, for five shillings per person, it was more than they could have bargained for.

They sat at the back in a trailer loaded with goods destined for some shops in Portuguese East Africa (Mozambique). Through patched vegetation and sometimes rollicking hill country, the truck raced on relentlessly, the driver intentionally wanting to get to his destination before sundown, before the forces of darkness began their stronghold on humanity in this part of the country that was so much renowned for its bizarre black magic. The truck driver stopped just once to stretch his cramped legs and allow his passengers to relieve themselves in the nearby bushes.

Their bottoms were sore from the constant jolting they had received when the truck ran over the numerous potholes on the rugged road. Nemon felt like his well padded bums were slowly losing their flesh and bones were getting nearer to the surface than they had been before. After a short rest, they resumed their journey, the driver increasing his speed a little, wanting to down a beer before the bars closed for the day. As they approached the Zambezi river, the vegetation began to change and the scenery turned to a beautiful rolling plain of thick savannah grass and big tall trees.

The driver dropped them off in town at the wholesale store he was making delivery to. They had already paid him the fare as they had covered the last miles of this leg.

The three young men from Mzimba mixed with the local Sena people and asked for directions to the nearest rest house where they could freshen up. They had not taken a bath since the day they had left home.

Finding the rest house proved to be easy and once they managed to communicate with the Portuguese owner, they paid for their boarding and were immediately shown into a big room teaming with travelers of all sorts.

Reed mats were laid on the floor and some people were already sleeping amidst the hubbub of noise. Nemon suggested they take turns in taking a bath so there always would be someone to look after their meager possessions.

Later, with everyone bathed and after having eaten some *nsima* and spicy fresh Zambezi bream fish, they settled in for the night. They were so beat up that not even the variably pitched snores of the more than hundred men and women and the incessant drone of the mosquitoes and their bites could wake them up from their deep, deep sleep.

11

When morning came, it was three men that woke up feeling rejuvenated and ready to take on the challenges of the world. They had a quick breakfast of porridge and some hard boiled eggs and as soon as they were done, they picked up their few belongings and headed for the river bank where the small dugout canoes had already started ferrying the people across the crocodile infested river.

Nemon and his two friends headed straight for one canoe that was festooned with bright colored ribbons and was about to launch off.

Nemon sat in the middle with strangers on either side of him. It was amazing how such a small traditional contraption could seat about twelve people and still be able to keep afloat.

Two rowers, one at either hand, dug their oars into the murky waters and began propelling the heavy laden boat into the deep African river. With each double stroke, they inched their way across the mile wide river. As they got to the center, one of Nemon's friends decided to fill his empty mazoe orange juice container with water.

Twisting off the cap, he let the mouth of the bottle drag across the top of the water, taking it in bit by bit.

The rower at the rear end yelled out something at him in his native Sena language which most people in the boat did not understand too well. However, the urgency in his voice was not lost to Nemon who turned around to see what the problem might be.

What happened next was so swift it was unbelievable. Those few moments would forever remain vividly etched in his mind for many years to come. The snorkel of big crocodile appeared out of nowhere and the gaping mouth closed on to the arm of his friend. One moment, he was there, the next, he was gone, the crunching sound of bone still reverberating in his head. Only the churning waters indicated the spot where reptile and man had plunged down in a desperate struggle to subdue and survive respectively.

That day belonged to the crocodile.

Everyone in the boat was stunned, shocked. The women began to scream but were quickly silenced by the stern looking oarsman.

When they got to the other side of the river and disembarked, Nemon's knees were like jelly.

He could hardly keep up on his feet. He sat down on the small patch of grass by the river bank, his heart burning with pain, tears running down his face.

How cruel mother nature could be at times, he thought to himself.

His remaining friend came and sat down beside him and, in silent communication, each knowing what the other felt, they clasped their hands together, letting their emotions take control. Tears bursting from an endless supply of unfathomable wells, they sang a Tumbuka hymn.

Para zuba lifinyi liza, ndakofya namphumu yikulu
Bangelo na batuba wose, kupoma nakululutila
Wamkuti, ku awo, balikuwoko lamaryelo
Zaninge, zaninge, muhale chihalo chandanda.

When that day cometh, so loud and frightening,
The angels and all the holly ones will sing and be happy.
And He will say to those on His right hand, come.
Come ye my children and inherit thine throne."

When they finished singing, Nemon said a short prayer and together, they threw the few belongings that had been their friend's into the river.

When they got a chance, they would write home and let the parents know how their friend had died.

They stood up and walked to where the big trucks stood loading up their cargo. They hoped to catch a ride on one that was headed to Harare via Chirundu.

12

Nemon's friend decided he was going to find work in Harare. After much deliberation, Nemon continued on his own to Bulawayo, to a people that spoke almost the same language as he did, reasoning that it would not be difficult to communicate with the locals there.

He boarded a bus at the Mbare market square the following morning and began what (he thought to himself) would be the final phase of his journey.

This was where his dreams would be realized, in the city where the smoke rose high into the sky thus earning itself the name of *'ko nthuthu ziyathunqa,'* where the smoke belches.

Late that afternoon, the bus drew into the Bulawayo bus terminus, popularly referred to as *'e renkini'*, and Nemon immediately set off into the nearby black residential area. He had a name and an address of one person living in the part of town known as "Old Location".

Asking some people on the way, he was given many misleading directions and after a couple of hours of diligent searching, he finally got to a house that bore the same number he had on a piece of paper.

Tentatively, he knocked on the door.

Getting no response, he knocked again, louder this time, his heart floundering, hoping against hope that this was the place he would find Masuzgo. He did not relish the thought of spending the night out on the streets.

At the third knock, almost a bang now, a sleepy eyed man opened the door and mumbled a greeting in heavy accented Ndebele. Nemon took in the man's fine features, the tall, lean and strong structure so reminiscent of his fellow tribesmen. He also noticed the ears pierced similarly to his own, big knife cuts on the lobes.

His spirits soared as he concluded this indeed was the person he sought. He returned the greeting in his native Nguni language and began to explain who he was and mentioned that he was looking for one Masuzgo Nyasulu.

Immediately the sleep vanished from the man's face and a warm smile spread from ear to ear.

It was not everyday that one opened the door to a visitor from the motherland.

"I am Masuzgo Nyasulu, please do come in and make yourself comfortable," the man invited Nemon in as he stepped back and opened the door wider.

After exchanging further formalities, Masuzgo asked briefly how the people at home were and how good the rains and crops had been this past season while he busied himself trying to prepare a hasty meal for his tired visitor.

Nemon explained in detail how much rain had fallen and how many granaries *(nkhokwe)* the people had filled with their crops of maize and groundnuts.

By the time food was ready, these two people that had never seen each other before, were like close pals.

Nemon offered to say a prayer before taking his meal and as soon as he said amen, Masuzgo took off from where he had left, grilling Nemon with question after question throughout the meal and way into the night.

When they both started yawning, Masuzgo suggested they turn in. Indicating to Nemon the spot where he could curl up, he gave him a threadbare blanket and, saying goodnight to each other, they both wrapped themselves up in their blankets in this small one roomed apartment.

This was it, Nemon said to himself before sleep overtook him. This was *'Harare'* and he had made it.

Silently, he said a prayer of thanks and gratitude to his maker and asked for guidance as he ventured out in this new land that the Lord had been so kind as to allow him come and try and realize his dreams.

And then, he slept.

13

Getting a job was easy for Nemon as Masuzgo had some friends working for the Railway company. They helped Nemon get a pass and took him to the recruiting offices at No. 2 compound and, three weeks after arriving in Bulawayo, he secured his first job.

He continued to live with Masuzgo until his third month of employment when he was provided with single accommodation by his employers at the No. 3 Compound complex. Showing his appreciation at having been well received and cared for, he assured Masuzgo of his lasting friendship and that he would forever be indebted to him.

With a meager monthly income of two pounds, ten shillings and six pence, Nemon managed to save enough money to send home come Christmas holidays. He worked hard at the nursery at Westgate where he tended all sorts of flowers, trees and shrubbery.

His first Christmas was spent with Masuzgo and some friends. The highlight of the day was the *Nguni ingoma* dance which was staged by ten men who had been dancing together for quite a while now. There were also some *malipenga* and *muganda* dances performed by some other groups, representing the diverse gathering of people from the small country of Nyasaland.

On his first anniversary at work, Nemon did not take time off to go home but opted to accrue the days so he would go on an extended break the following year and, maybe, with a substantial amount of money and some gifts for his family.

So, come September of 1939, Nemon applied for two months' leave and, toting two heavy leaden suitcases and about sixty pounds in cash, he set off on his journey back home to his family which he had not seen for over two years.

14

It was a balmy day when Nemon got off the bus at Emoneni. Far gone was the strutting young man that had left this village with nothing more than the clothes on his back and a small pouch of food in his hands. He was resplendent in a gray suit, blue shirt and brown striped tie that matched his new shining shoes.

Beckoning one of the boys that had come to watch the bus come and go by, Nemon asked the boy to help him carry the extra suitcase and promised him some monetary reward.

They made the descent into the valley towards his village, stopping several times on the way to adjust their grips on the heavy suitcases, changing them from one hand to the other, till they reached the first cluster of huts.

Here, Nemon thanked the boy and gave him a crown (two shilling and six pence coin). Word spread quickly that he was back and when it reached his house, his wife came shooting out as if propelled by rocket fire.

She ran and embraced him, shouting out in joy. Jenara picked up the one suitcase and put it on her head and urged Nemon to leave the other as Siphiwe would come to carry it.

Timidly, Siphiwe appeared, no longer a small girl but a young woman. She had changed a lot during the two or so years that Nemon had been away. She knelt down at a distance and greeted her father as custom dictated. At her age, she was no longer allowed to talk at length with her father let alone make any physical contact.

Nemon let his daughter carry the second suitcase while he followed behind.

His dad came out, an old man, using a wood carved cane, his back doubled, the result of having toiled too long in the fields. They hugged and shook hands.

They sat down, father and son, in the shaded porch of Nemon's house and exchanged greetings, the father marveling at how well his son looked, the son feeling pity for a father made to look older than his age due to the rigours of a peasant life lived day in and day out all year round.

They enquired of each other's health and discussed the rains and the crops and general things concerning relatives and other people in the village.

Nemon's mother, Nya Mpande, as his dad affectionately called her, rushed over to her son and knelt on the ground before him, looking him in the eyes. She clasped his right hand in both her hands and shook it vigorously, asking him how he was, all the time interjecting, "*Nadi, mwiza sambiri*. You really came back to us, I can't believe it".

Before long, most of the villagers had come to welcome back home one of their sons.

Later on, when Nemon had bathed and changed, he sat down with his wife and was updated on all family matters.

Early into the night, he took out his gifts and handed them to his wife, daughter, parents and aunt.

They talked away into the wee hours of the morning before Nemon begged to get some sleep.

The following morning, after breakfast, Nemon took it upon himself to go visit the parents of his friend that had been killed by the crocodile on the Zambezi river. Accompanied by his wife, he took with him gifts of clothing for both the mother and the father. When he got there, he offered his condolences and explained to them in detail what had happened on that fateful day. He agreed to having a bit of his favorite drink, *mahewu*, but declined the offer to stay for a meal. The woman ordered some kids to catch a fowl which she presented to Nemon.

Nemon thanked them both and, with his wife carrying the chicken, they departed and headed home.

That evening, a variety of foods came in from most of the neighbours but Nemon settled for the dish of chicken and *sima* that his wife had prepared. The meal was served on the verandah of his father's house.

After supper, he was further updated by his wife and parents of all the events that had happened transpired during his absence. They laughed at some funny things and commiserated on the sad ones. Deciding they would continue discussions the following day, Nemon and Jenara said goodnight and left for their house.

It was to be a night of conjugal duty, so long put aside by the absence from one another.

15

Early into the second month of his stay at home, Jenara advised Nemon that she had missed her period. At about the same time she developed conjuctivitis, forcing her to spend most of her time indoors away from the sun. The tetracycline eye ointment that Nemon bought from the SDA mission dispensary at Mombera (Mbelwa) helped for a little while.

As soon as she ran out, however, the problem resuscitated. In the end, they settled for going to Ekwendeni hospital for treatment.

Jenara was hospitalized for a week and her condition monitored closely until she was discharged. The doctors gave her lots of antibiotic eye ointment that she could use in case of further infection.

Nemon and his wife took advantage of the little time they had and visited a few friends and relatives before catching the bus back to Emoneni.

Nemon was forced to extend his stay till his wife's health improved. He helped with the preparation of the fields, tilling the land in anticipation of the rains.

Just as Nemon was deciding on returning to Southern Rhodesia back to work, his wife fell sick again, passing out on several occasions due to a persistent headache. Her vision became affected, blurring from time to time.

Despite the analgesics she got from the dispensary, the headaches never abated. Reluctantly, Nemon agreed for his wife to be treated by a traditional healer.

Using a new razor blade, the medicine man pinched the flesh and made several small cuts on either side of Jenara's face, applying some black soot to the cuts so it could be absorbed into the blood stream.

Producing some fresh bark from the *mubabani* tree, he dipped it into a small pot with water and advised the patient to drink from it two times a day, each time replenishing the water.

It was quite amazing what happened thereafter.

After a week of treatment, Jenara reported she was feeling much better. Her fainting spells disappeared and her vision improved. When the medicine man returned after a month for a *'follow up consultation'*, Nemon insisted that he accept the gift of a goat.

Nemon's spirits buoyed up as he saw his three month pregnant wife resume her normal routine.

Early December, the rains came and Nemon decided he might as well spend Christmas with his family. He was sure his supervisors would understand and let him keep his job once he got back to Rhodesia.

Everyone went out to prepare their fields and sow their maize and bean seeds. With Nemon's assistance, Jenara increased her acreage and prayed her harvest this time would be unprecedented.

A week before Christmas, a group of people from Manola came into the homestead and aunt Balekile announced to Nemon and Jenara that they had come to ask for Siphiwe's hand in marriage.

It came both as a shock and surprise for the young parents. Although they had realized that their daughter had grown up to be a young woman, it had not crossed their minds that she could be eligible for marriage so soon.

At fourteen years, Siphiwe stood a few inches taller than her frail looking mother.

A gathering of the elders was called for and the matter discussed. In the end it was decided that these people come back at a later date in January when they would be told how much *lobola* (dowry) they would need to bring with them.

Christmas came and went.

The rains were aplenty and the crop grew healthy. All over, the fields looked nice and green. The people went out to weed the fields and they were more than pleased with the way the crop was coming up.

If the rains continued as they did, Nemon thought, they would have a bumper harvest. New year was hardly celebrated. It did not mean anything to them. They continued with their various duties as usual.

On the second Saturday of January, the people from Manola came again and, after a short pow-wow, they were advised that they would need to pay four cows for *lobola*.

They promised to be back the following weekend, which they did, driving in four healthy looking cows, one of them about to calf.

The wedding *(zowala)* date was set for 17 March, 1940 and frivolous preparations began to be made to ensure that, when Siphiwe went away to her new home, she would have everything she might require.

Nemon had so far resigned himself to going back to work once he'd given his daughter away. He was not going to miss his only child's wedding.

As the day of the zowala drew nearer, most of the villagers joined in making the final arrangements of what would be Nemon and Jenara's first experience.

On the eve of the big day, with people gathering and preparing for an early start for Manola the following morning, Siphiwe started to complain of a headache and retired early.

Everyone concluded it was the jitters and anxiety she must have been experiencing.

When morning came, the elders were aroused by some screaming and crying by the girls from Siphiwe's *nthanganeni.*

The women rushed out to investigate the cause of this alarm and were absolutely in shock when they discovered what had happened.

Siphiwe lay still on her reed mat, her blanket pulled down to her waist, a smile on her face, her eyes closed. She had died peacefully in her sleep.

What was supposed to have been a wedding extravaganza turned out to be a funeral procession instead.

They buried Siphiwe late in the afternoon, decorating her grave with some of the gifts they had intended to present to her on her special day.

Nemon and Jenara, so accustomed to strange happenings in their family, could not take this unexpected blow. They both grieved very deeply. All the painful memories that had been carefully shoved away resurfaced and fueled their emotions, leaving them helpless and bursting out in anguish.

If ever they needed support, this was the time they most needed it, and they never lacked it.

Friends and relatives came to pay their condolences, even their prospective in-laws and relatives from Manola came in as well.

Especially helpful and supportive were Nemon's fellow Christian friends. His cousin, now the Reverend Hara, came in from Ekwendeni to comfort him.

These people took them through the most difficult stage they had ever faced in their lives.

Gradually, the intense pain they felt within themselves began to dissipate as they came to accept the loss of their only child.

The Lord had given and the Lord had taken.

Two weeks after the burial, the whole family and some close relatives sat down and discussed issues pertaining to the marriage that had never come to be.

It was decided by the majority of the people there, that the cows intended as dowry payment for the late Siphiwe be returned to the Kamangas'. Three people were appointed to drive the herd back and to offer condolences to the Kamanga family.

Meanwhile, Jenara made a surprisingly quick recovery, going about her duties as usual, her pregnancy not a hindrance anyhow. Late into her term, Nemon asked her to take it easy while he took care of most of the chores around the house.

On June 12, 1940, Jenara gave birth to a baby girl whom they immediately named *Phyela*, meaning *'swept clean with nothing remaining'*.

All their children had been swept away and devoured by some unknown phenomenon. They did not have a single child soul in their household.

After a few weeks in isolation from the outside world, as tradition required, the baby was allowed to be taken out of the house into the sunlight and the public.

Nemon contemplated taking his wife with him to Rhodesia, but soon discarded the idea knowing this would be a burden on his wife and his aging parents.

However, at four months, his daughter fell sick and for a time, it was touch and go. When the baby's condition improved, all vacillating was put aside and he made immediate arrangements to depart with his family.

So, one day into early November, Nemon and his wife bade farewell to their parents, friends and relatives and began the long arduous journey to Harare, a move that probably saved Phyela's life.

16

Nemon did not have any problem getting his job back. He was, however, sent to work in the steam shed. The housing department allocated him some family accommodation at No. 3 Compound while Compound No. 5 was being constructed.

Jenara and the baby received medical attention at the Westgate clinic and the baby got all her immunizations.

During the weekends that he was free, Nemon and his family visited his friend Masuzgo Nyasulu and on Sundays, they got together with some other people from Mzimba and worshipped under the shadow of a big tree.

Nemon became actively involved in these Sunday gatherings and worship. When more and more people came to join them, he suggested they look for a bigger place that could accommodate the growing congregation. The majority of the worshippers came from the northern region of Malawi and had attended school at one of the many schools set up by the Livingstonia mission.

A few people from the central and southern regions of Malawi also joined and, from a small gathering of fifteen people, their membership grew to over two hundred.

At one of the elders' meetings, it was decided that they seek permission from the city authorities so that they could use one of the classrooms of a local school as a place of worship.

For a nominal fee of five shillings per month, this request was granted. Nemon was one of the eight original members that had initially started this worship group and so the foundation of the CCAP in Bulawayo was set up.

His family did well too. His wife's eye problem was treated by the experienced physicians at the Nazareth Health Center. Phyela grew up healthy and strong. She was full of energy, playing with the other children and grasping the Ndebele language very fast.

In 1946 and 1949, Nemon and Jenara were blessed with two baby boys and they named them Moses and Frank respectively.

The sound of children's voices once again echoed within the walls of the Gumbo house. The health of the children became a major concern and they were closely monitored. There was no hesitation whatsoever in visiting the doctor when slight symptoms of illness cropped up.

When Nemon received the news of the death of his parents, he was not able to travel to Malawi. Friends gathered at his home and prayed with him and offered him all the comfort they could.

Prayer was a constant thing in this household. This was a God loving house and with the Lord's blessings they prospered.

For the first time, Nemon and Jenara watched their children slowly grow into adulthood.

With everything going well, and the congregation growing larger and larger, some monetary contributions were made for a church to be built.

Together with the money from the Sunday offerings, the first CCAP church was built in Nguboyenja in the late fifties.

It was in this church that their daughter Phyela (now known as Fainess), aged eighteen, was married to Faiton Tembo, a grandson of Rev. Mawelela Tembo.

The Rev. Du Toit, sent in from the Dutch Reformed Church in South Africa, conducted the ceremony. It was a happy occasion and a milestone for these two parents that had known so much pain and had been through the most trying periods no average person ever experienced in a lifetime.

And so, to her new home Fainess went on that cold day of June 1958. A daughter had been lost, but more so, a son had been gained.

Two months after getting married, Fainess conceived and everyone was excited, the newlyweds eager to have their first born child, Nemon and Jenara on the other hand, expectant grandparents, very eager to see their first grandchild.

17

Thursday morning, April 16 1959, Phyela was rushed to Mpilo Hospital by ambulance after she reported to Jenara she was having cramps.

Late that afternoon, she gave birth to a bouncy healthy baby boy.

Perhaps her going into labor had been induced by news she had received eighteen hours earlier. The post man had delivered a telegram to her house and being afraid to open it by herself, she had taken it to her parents' house so her father could open it for her.

The telegram bore bad news. Her husband had died of malaria about three days earlier. The news had hit her real hard. She'd felt numb, her body suddenly a mass of boneless flesh, unable to obey even the simplest of commands. Feeling faint and on the verge of collapse, she had sat down on the ground, clutching her stomach which had suddenly registered the onset of labor activity. It was a difficult time for her.

A time to mourn a dearly loved companion so suddenly snatched away from her on one hand, and, on the other, a time to rejoice for the gift of a precious life.

It was an end and a beginning.

Her husband had left for Malawi on compassionate leave after he had received news of the death of his father. Being the only son, it had fallen upon him to bear all family responsibilities and ensure that the family's wealth of countless head of cattle would not be plundered by greedy relatives.

Faiton had left Malawi six years earlier to look for work in the mines of Zimbabwe. After having worked briefly for the Wankie Colliery Company, unable to cope with the unrelenting heat, he had moved down to Bulawayo where he had landed a job with the Rhodesia Railway Company.

He had managed to send his parents some money each month so they could purchase some livestock and beef up the small herd of cattle they already possessed. On a couple of occasions, before he had met his wife, Faiton had been to visit his parents and he had been quite pleased to see that they were doing really well. The herd of cattle had tripled and the old man had even begun to rear some goats.

On his next visit, he had planned to take his wife and soon to be born child with him to meet his parents.

However, the news of his father's death had put paid all those plans and he had immediately packed a few things and left for Njuyu alone with a heavy heart and tears in his eyes, not knowing what fate had in store for him.

The short, brief, too brief a telegram, received that Wednesday afternoon had just said that Faiton had died of malaria on April 12, 1959.

By the time it was delivered to the addressee at the small asbestos house of No. 5 compound, Faiton had already been buried for three days in that faraway land.

When Fainess left hospital two days later with her kid wrapped in a soft blue blanket, it was to return to a house full of grieving relatives and friends.

Here she was, young, confused and feeling lost.

What did the world expect her to do? How was she supposed to react to this? How was she going to cope by herself?

All she felt was a sense of foreboding, of helplessness, feeling she had been unfairly treated by her gods and ancestral spirits. At a tender age of eighteen, she was already a widow before she'd even reared a family.

For a week, the people remained in mourning until the following Saturday when, as tradition required, Fainess' head was shaved clean and she put on a black dress as a symbol of her grieving status.

After the many rituals, the people dispersed and her house turned deadly silent.

She found comfort in her mother's company. Jenara stayed with her day and night, caring for her and her newly born child, repeatedly assuring her that everything would be all right.

Despite the small measure of comfort, Fainess often broke down into uncontrollable fits of quiet painful crying, tears streaming down her face like water from a dysfunctional faucet.

Her body would shake as she tried desperately to contain the pain and anger so heavy in her heart, a solid like mound of painful mass that never melted despite the continuous outpour of tears. It was like a tear on a piece of fabric, an irreparable tear.

It took Jenara some time to talk sense into her and help her emerge out of this surreal painful world.

Her eating habits changed and, as a result, she did not produce enough breast milk for the baby. The baby, perhaps sensing the helplessness nature of the mother, homed in onto the grandmother's maternal nature and refused to be tended to by its biological mother.

He refused to suckle from the breast thus prompting Jenara to buy him a feeding bottle. And so it was, that from a very tender age, I began to regard my grandmother as my mother. My grandparents were father and mother to me and we developed a very close bond with each other. My two uncles were like my brothers and no one could doubt that.

When Fainess remarried two years later, no mother-son bond existed between us.

To me No. 5 compound was a shanty complex that seemed to have been put up in too much of a hurry so as to provide cheap accommodation for the many native migrant workers from Malawi, Zambia, Tanzania and Zaire.

Better accommodation was built in 1963 in the new townships called Sizinda and Tshabalala. Everyone was moved to the new complex in tractor loads and for the first time, we had piped water right in the houses.

I grew up a healthy boy in a strict Christian family and by the tender age of four, I could recite some verses from the scriptures.

This was a God fearing household.

I went to Maphisa Primary School and later on graduated and attended Mpopoma High School.

I was having the time of my life until that day when grandpa announced to the family he'd been recommended to retire on health grounds. He did not say much but indicated he had put much thought into it and had decided that he would take his pension and go back to Malawi.

18

On one of granddad's many visits to Ekwendeni, he had come back a sick person. Despite being hospitalized at Mpilo hospital, there was very little improvement to his condition. Taking another month long vacation, both grandma and grandpa returned to Malawi to seek traditional remedies for his condition.

Upon his return it was quite apparent that nothing had been achieved from this visit. Whatever it was that was ailing him was taking its toll on this once healthy man.

When he no longer could perform his duties satisfactorily, an appointment was set up with the Railway Medical Officer so as to have his health evaluated. It was at this time that a recommendation was made that he retire on medical grounds. So, in May of 1975, grandpa retired and made arrangements to return to his village of Ekwendeni.

His congregation was very supportive. The gifts that he received were too many for him to pack and take with him. Uncle Frank and myself escorted grandma and grandpa to the Harare International Airport where they boarded a plane to Malawi.

With a heavy rock in my heart, I watched them board the Air Zimbabwe plane that would take them away from me to that country that I'd never been to myself. Although I tried to remain calm and relaxed, the pain within me was unbearable.

I had lived my whole life with these two people and, suddenly, they were leaving me alone with my uncles. I felt lost, confused and somewhat discarded. My whole world literally fell apart.

My grades in school started dropping and my performance became pathetic.

It was a long school term for me. When I was unfairly punished by the principal for something I had not done, I decided I'd had enough and wanted out of school.

I asked my uncles to make arrangements for me so I could go join my grandparents. So, when schools closed in August, I bade farewell to my friends and prepared for the long journey to Malawi, the so called "Warm Heart of Africa."

19

The Frelimo government had just come into power in Mozambique when I started off for Malawi. I journeyed by train through the war ravaged country. It was a slow journey with constant stops and searches by the over zealous young Frelimo soldiers.

From Machipanda border post to Dondo, the railway line snaked around mountainous terrain.

I spent the night at Dondo station and boarded the train from Beira the following morning, running all day long to Villa Nova. We detrained there and proceeded through some immigration formalities.

Another restless night was spent out in the open at the mercy of thousands of gigantic mosquitoes that bred in the marshes of the nearby Zambezi river.

We crossed the Zambezi in the morning, the train packed with the locals, most of them fishmongers on their way to the border town of Nsanje to sell their catches.

Four days after catching the train at Machipanda, I finally got to Limbe. Catching buses to Lilongwe, Mzimba and eventually Ekwendeni was relatively easy.

I got to Ekwendeni after another two days of being subjected to the most bumpy ride I had ever had on some of the worst roads I'd ever seen. I was totally worn out. My bums ached so much it felt like all the flesh had been ripped off.

Heavy suitcase in hand, I asked for directions to grandpa's village. It took me forty minutes to get there and when grandma saw me, she flew at me, hugged and kissed me.

I had arrived at last.

This place looked like a scene out of a Tarzan movie.

On hearing the commotion outside, grandpa came out of the house, a smile on his face. We hugged and I let the tears roll down my face unashamedly.

These were the two people that I got on very well with. With them by my side, what more on earth could I have wanted. I was very content.

We sat down on the verandah and recapped on events covering the period since we'd last seen each other. It felt very good to be back together with my parents.

After a week of rest, I made my way to the Ministry of Education in Mzuzu to apply for a place at any one of their schools.

Politics reared its ugly head and put to rest my plans to further my education. The authorities in the Education ministry refused to grant me a place in any of their schools insisting that I renounce my Rhodesian citizenship first.

I was taken aback. Here I was, a child of sixteen being drawn into a political mire. I told them I was not ready to give away my birth rights, never.

Failing to get them to change their minds, I eventually settled for a clerical job at Ekwendeni CCAP Hospital, becoming the youngest member of staff.

It is at this hospital that grandpa was constantly hospitalized. Here I had the opportunity to work with probably the best surgeon that ever worked in this central African country. Dr. Kenneth Irvine was an epitome of Jesus' disciples in both his work conduct and also the spread of gospel within the community. Patients came in from as far as Tanzania and Zambia to be treated by him at this ill equipped missionary hospital. Referrals were sometimes received from some of the big city hospitals and this Scottish doctor did his best to treat all.

If ever the Good Lord manifested Himself in human beings, He shone in this man. Never has one person touched the lives of so many people in this region as did Dr. Irvine. He spoke the native Tumbuka language better than the locals themselves and his spoken Ngoni was lovely to hear. Each time he stood at the pulpit to deliver a sermon, it was a fulfilling experience to hear him.

When he suddenly passed away a few years later while on leave in Scotland, his remains were flown back to Ekwendeni as per his request, and buried there.

The whole nation mourned. The church was full to the brim with people from all walks of life. The rich and the poor, the disabled and the able bodied all came to pay their respects to this good man of God. Even the media from the nation's daily paper came to cover the funeral proceedings.

This is the man I had the privilege to rub shoulders with. Together with another Irish doctor, Anne E Watts, I was groomed into an administration position.

I was also encouraged to take up accounting studies with the auditing department of the Synod of Livingstonia. It was, in fact, Dr. Watts that helped me pay for my examination fees when I eventually sat for my examinations with the University of Cambridge. Working with these caring missionaries played a big part in shaping up my adult life.

With the guidance of grandpa at home and that of these expatriates at work, I learnt to be a more caring, loving and understanding person.

As time went by, I grew stronger in mind and spirit.

I became the head of the Hospital Christian Fellowship and shared the good news with lots of patients and fellow workers.

We held services in the different wards of the hospital and brought the word of God to the many people who had not been saved.

It is true that there were more people going through the hospitals than to the churches and it was important that some of these dying people be at least given the opportunity to hear the saving word of God.

However, my concern for grandpa never wavered. Each time he fell sick, I had him picked up and brought to the hospital where Dr. Irvine tended him.

During periods when his health improved and his strength returned, I would take time off from work and we visited all places where he still had some relatives.

We went to Eswazini to meet the Sibandas, to Mombera and Emoneni, meeting many people, most of them surprised that I could speak the language of their ancestors, the Zulu language.

I think it was my ability to speak the Nguni language that made me make friends with the elders of the village.

Toward the end of 1976, grandpa's health deteriorated rapidly and despite specialized care, he did not really improve.

He would be home for only a short while before he would relapse again and I'd be forced to take him back to hospital.

20

Ten years later, I sit in the very same old leather thonged couch on the reconstructed verandah and can almost hear grandpa's voice as he had related his story to me.

It had taken him almost three days to narrate his life's story.

I smile to myself and wonder what we could have been discussing today were he still alive.

As I look across the village, past a cluster of sun baked brick houses, most of them sporting corrugated iron roofing sheets, I catch a glimpse of the recently tended graves of my grandparents, the bright yellow and pink flowers catching the late morning sunlight.

Earlier in the morning, my wife, son, daughter and myself had worked on the graves which had been overgrown with shrubs from several years of neglect.

This is the first time my family has been to Malawi. It was important for me to bring them here and show them where my parents lie buried.

I know, wherever they are, that they must have been pleased to see my small family gather around their graves and sing a Tumbuka hymn and pray for their souls to rest in peace.

Today, a thousand miles away from our home in Boston, Massachusetts, here we were, in this small village of Ekwendeni, sharing, as we always did, a bit of my old past.

I recall what had happened that day when I had finally taken a spade and hoe to dig my grandfather's grave on that bleak day of March 30, 1977.

I can't help but smile as snippets of our discussions come to mind, mostly words of advice that cropped up in almost every conversation we had, words said in such a way as would be easily remembered and plucked from the recesses of my brain.

"Remember to always do good for others as your deeds will follow you throughout the days of your life," he would say, "and share with others in need whatever it is that they ask of you and you have it, no matter how small it might be."

I can not help but let the tears pour down my eyes as the pain wells up within me. I remember clearly the events leading to grandpa's death. So vivid is the memory it seems it might have happened just yesterday.

21

It had started the day before and grandma had known for certain that something bad was going to happen. For the second time since I'd been working at the hospital, I missed work due to a pain in my right shoulder. I woke up feeling something burning just below the shoulder blade. As I tried to reach for the spot with my left hand, the pain became so unbearable I immediately jumped out of bed. I looked in on grandpa to see if he was awake. He was fast asleep. I left his room quietly making sure not to disturb him. He had coughed continuously during the night, those heart rending coughs that produced no sputum at all but played havoc to his chest. At times, when he could bear the pain no longer, he would ask that I tie some piece of cloth tight around his chest. That seemed to help, somehow. I headed straight to the outside cooking hut where a plume of smoke was coming out of the thatched roof. I ducked my head into the smoke filled interior and said hello to my grandma. She'd already been to the river to fetch some water.

" Hello honey, aren't you going to work today?" she asked me as she tried to coax the fire by blowing hard at the ambers. She was preparing some maize porridge cooked with fresh goat milk.

"I am not feeling too good grandma," I replied.

"I have this funny pain in my back and it's making my arm stiff" I informed her.

"Are you sure you did not sleep on it son?" she continued as she stood up, placing the wooden spoon she'd been using into the maize-meal basket.

I backed out into the sunlight so she could have a very good look at this small swelling on my back. I took off my shirt and indicated the spot where the pain was.

"Well, well, well, well, what is this we have here?" she began.

"It looks like you have been bitten by some insect," she went on while gently probing the area like a qualified physician.

I knew she was a good medicine woman as was evidenced by the number of people that came to seek treatment from her. At times, the queues resembled those of people waiting at a pharmacy to have their prescriptions filled.

She was good at helping infertile couples and was also the village midwife. Some of her herbs were good for treatment of malaria and sexually transmitted diseases.

I did not try any of her concoctions as I could not stand the very potent dosages she usually dispensed to her patients, most of the drugs taken in big mugs and wooden plates.

Whatever my sentiments were, it seemed her patients were satisfied with the results and always passed on a good word to the next person who might have been suffering from a similar ailment.

Come to think of it, she never used to charge her patients any fee. They usually brought her gifts of chicken, mealie-meal, melons and occasionally a goat once they were cured of their afflictions.

Despite her wide knowledge of African herbs, she was not able to come up with a cure for grandpa's illness. I remember one night when she had walked in her sleep, covering a distance of about twelve miles, crossing the Lunyangwa river and going to a hill in Enyezini to get a particular herb she used to treat a child with epileptic seizures. She said later on that she'd been led by some spirit and the little kid never experienced another attack after her treatment.

"Looks like you may need some aspiration, young man," she said as she gently squeezed the base of the swollen area.

"This looks like it is ready to burst," she commented, "just remain calm and relaxed while I squeeze out whatever is inside," she drooled on.

There was no clinical method, no gloves and no swabbing alcohol.

She went straight to work and I braced myself and tried to ride the pain as she squeezed real hard, forcing the skin to break.

"Wow, look at this," she exclaimed as she applied more pressure to the affected area.

"I have only seen this once in my whole life and it can only mean bad news", she said as a matter of fact.

"Take a good look at this", she said as I turned around to see what it was she proclaimed brought bad tidings and had affected my grandma so much her voice had turned tremulous and dropped almost to a whisper.

There, on her chapped fingernail, wriggled two small larvae.

I could not fathom how on earth these things could have gotten into my body. A chill ran down my spine as I imagined festering flesh.

She ground the two parasites to death with the use of another fingernail from her other thumb.

Bad omen or not, I knew what I needed to do.

A bottle of Dettol disinfectant was all I needed. I quickly thanked her for her services and put on my shirt. I went into the house and got out my bicycle, determined to get to the shops as quickly as I could so I could purchase the disinfectant and some antiseptic lotion.

I was not taking any chances. I covered the four mile distance to the stores in record time, deftly maneuvering the big Phillips bicycle along the narrow path down toward the stream that separated the village from the mission station, up the hill past the MCC center, eventually joining the main tarred road from Mzuzu that ran behind the new Ekwendeni Girls Secondary School on to the shopping complex that consisted of several grocery shops, the market, Post Office, Chipiku Wholesalers and an array of bakeries.

The whiff of freshly baked bread came to my nose and I made a mental note to get a loaf before going back home. I rested my bike against a pole on the awning of Chimutanda and Sons Store and walked into the store to make my purchases. I asked for a cold bottle of fanta and two cream doughnuts for my improptu breakfast and also asked for two bottles of Dettol. I took my time eating my food while discussing the morning weather with one of the store attendants, keeping a watchful eye on my bike all the time.

I later on bought two loaves of bread and got onto my bike and made my way back home.

This time I took the longer route, cycling up the main road towards Ekwaliweni, toward Chinungu hill, past Mapemba's grinding mill already packed with loud voiced women, up to the Chibambos' homestead, taking a right turn there that would bring me past the Kawongas and on to our house from the eastern side of the village.

When I got home, I could hear grandpa coughing as soon as I walked in through the door.

He was sitting up in bed with grandma atttending to him.

It was as always, that wrecking cough that left him breathless and gasping for air, never giving him any respite. Grandma had tied a piece of cloth around his chest but that did not seem to be helping anyhow today. To compound matters further, he was bleeding through the nose into a bowl he held in his hands, a steady drip of blood that never abated despite the cold compress that grandma applied to his forehead and nose bridge.

The bleeding came to a stop after ten minutes and I took the bowl from his hands and went out to the pit latrine at the back of the house to empty it.

I rinsed out the bowl with hot water which grandma had boiling on the fire in the cooking hut and brought it back into the house just in case the bleeding resumed.

I sat down on the bed next to this gentle old man, noticing how he was struggling not to let the pain show on his face.

It hurt me so much that this man of God should have to suffer so much despite the advances made by science in the field of medicine.

Could not a cure be found for this one man?

I had gotten down on my knees several times and asked the Lord to cure this man. Maybe I just did not have faith enough. Maybe the Lord took his time answering some prayers or, maybe this time His answer was a plain "No".

We looked at each other, my face full of emotional pain, his with the physical pain he tried to downplay. I remembered how he had always said to me since I was a little boy.

"Son, you are the one that is going to bury me" he would say.

Deep within me, I could feel his prediction was going to be true.

"I pray each day," he gasped, "for the Lord to take my soul. I don't know why I have to suffer like this", he continued.

Here was a man of faith like no other I had ever seen before. On several occasions when everything seemed lost, he would seek solace in the Bible. He read the whole book of Job and said to me his faith would remain strong, just like Job's, no matter what pain he endured. He would rather have died in faith.

When his coughing subsided, I asked him if he wanted me to serve him with his porridge. He ate sparingly, only a few spoonfuls.

He was so tired he decided he was going to lay back and rest. He dozed and was soon sleeping with a light wheezing sound escaping through his slightly open mouth.

I went outside and assured grandma everything would be okay and that she should go on with her intended plans for the day and I would look after grandpa.

The rains came down that afternoon. First a steady shower so reminiscent of the Mzuzu area and the Viphya plateau weather, then, suddenly, a heavy deluge that produced a loud din on the iron roof sheets of the un-ceilinged house.

Strangely enough, the resultant noise and the thunder brought with it that melancholy effect of drifting away into a deep and peaceful slumber.

Earlier on, I had prepared lunch for grandpa and myself. After the meal we had talked a bit and I had read a passage for him from the Scriptures from his Zulu bible that he prized so much, a gift from my uncle.

We had discussed the contents and after a while, I had suggested that he get some rest.

I began to get concerned about grandma who had gone to check on her fields on the other side of the river.

Making sure grandpa was comfortable, I got into my bed and began to read my Louis L'amour western novel. I must have read about two chapters before my eyes became heavy and I fell asleep.

I woke to the sound of grandma making a ruckus and talking loudly to herself. She had developed this habit which I found to be very strange. She would sometimes go on and on and one would have thought she was conversing with another person. The older my grandma got the more strange the habits she developed.

I got out of bed, put my novel aside, and went out to interrupt this one sided conversation.

I followed grandma to the cooking hut where she was trying to get a fire going. She was soaked to the skin.

I told her not to worry as there was enough paraffin in the pressure stove to prepare more than one meal with.

I advised her to get into some dry clothes and not to bother about cooking as I would do that. I brewed her a cup of very hot Tanganda tea and served it to her in her favorite kango mug. I made some butter and jam sandwiches to go with the tea.

I made an extra cup for grandpa who had woken up by this time and was complaining he was feeling cold.

I sat in a chair and watched the two old people sip their hot beverage. Grandma related to us how her day had fared. As it got darker, I lit the hurricane lamp and proceeded to prepare a simple meal of nsima and dried fish.

As grandma was feeling worn out, we had our evening prayers much earlier than usual and we all retired to bed. With the rain still falling, I got into bed and blew out my lamp. No sooner had my head touched the pillow than I was out.

22

The rains must have stopped falling during the night. When morning came and the sky cleared, there was some freshness in the air, some kind of purity that one could draw into the lungs with each breath taken. The grass was bent from the force of the rain and the gentle wind.

I made my way to the pit latrine behind the house to relieve myself and started the fire in grandma's cooking hut. I heated up some bathing water in the big water can. I was feeling good this morning but strangely enough, did not feel like going to work at all.

Sitting alone in the small kitchen, I pondered on what to do next. The one part of me wanted me to go to work while the other strongly urged me to go jump back into my bed.

I cast the deciding vote, siding with the part of me that did not want to go to work.

With the water heated up, I poured it into a big dish, cooled it down a little to the desired temperature, and gave myself a quick rub down.

I heated up some more water for grandma and grandpa and went into the house to tell them the water was ready.

Already, people were going about their business, most of them (toting) their long handled hoes on their way to the fields. The children in their bright blue uniforms were jogging to school. They had to be there before the toll of the church bell or else they were sure to undergo some punishment. It was a very strict missionary school they went to.

Grandma came out to the cooking hut and greeted me.

"How have you woken up today, mother?" I said the traditional good morning greeting.

"I am alright son, just worried about the old man. He does not look good at all" she said as she ducked and went into the little hut.

I went back into the house and made straight for grandpa and grandma's bedroom from where I could hear his wheezing breath.

The look on his face told me he was in immense pain. He could hardly respond to my greeting. He laboured to say a few words and I felt something in me giving way.

The tears welled up in my eyes as he looked at me and managed a weak smile.

"Son, remember what I have taught you. Remember all I have said to you," he said with much difficuflty, "and take good care of your mother", he concluded.

Yes, I remembered. I remembered everything he'd shared with me from the tender age of six when I started to show a little bit of sense. I knew exactly what he was referring to.

I nodded my head slowly, letting the tears run down my face freely. In his way, he was simply confirming to me that he knew his time was up.

"Most of all," he continued, "remember what I have told you about this place since you've been here."

I held his hand in mine and just looked at him, acknowledging what he was saying. I wished then that I was a doctor. I would have dedicated my service to finding a cure for this man that I adored so much.

That morning, March 30, 1977, he could not get out of bed for his morning bath. Taking a face towel, grandma gave him a bed bath like they did to bed-bound patients in hospital. He was not even able to eat his breakfast either, complaining of some clamping pain in his chest.

Here I was, helpless, unable to render any kind of assistance, except hold onto his clammy and sweaty hand.

When grandma came in, he looked at both of us with a grin on his face.

"I would like to go and die in my own house. Are you able to carry me there?" he asked with a smile.

I told him the builders had just plastered the walls the previous day and it would still be wet and cold. It did not matter to him. All he wanted to do was expire within the walls of his own house.

Grandma did not argue. She knew she had to fulfill grandpa's wishes, this man that she had known for over fifty years.

They'd been through a lot together and had stood together side by side through thick and thin.

"Son, please go ask Silo to come over quickly", she instructed me.

Levi Silo was grandpa's good friend. I ran to his house and brought him out in a rush.

Silo looked at his old friend and they seemed to communicate without words being spoken.

"Nemon, I pray that you go in peace. Let the Lord take this pain away from you," he said.

Grandpa looked at him and smiled. The three of us helped him out of bed onto the three seater couch and laid him down gently.

Covering him with a bed sheet, we carried him out on the sofa and started for the new house that stood about a hundred yards away.

Halfway to his new house, between those tall jacaranda and syringa trees that cast a cool shadow on the narrow path, the same path he had taken so many years ago with his friend Aramson when he'd gone to visit Jenara, grandpa reached out his right hand and shook grandma's hand, a handshake that said a lot.

"Thank you for the good times we shared. Please take care. I love you and I will always love you."

I knew what that handshake said and so did grandma.

With a smile on his face, his spirit departed and grandma gently pulled down the eyelids over his staring eyes.

Miraculously, we all kept our composure until we placed his body on the bed in what would have been his bedroom. We covered his body with a blanket and then grandma broke down.

I could not believe that grandpa could have died so easily, gone in an instant, his breath snatched away. I had to make sure he was not in a coma or something.

It must have been a record four mile sprint I did that day. I completely forgot about the bicycle I possessed. I think back now and guess it must have been shock that had gotten the better of me.

I made it to the Hospital in less that eight minutes, quickly located Dr. Irvine and explained to him what had happened.

Grabbing his bag, we jumped into the ambulance and raced back to the village.

He shook his head as he examined the still body of this person he had treated for a long time.

"He is no more," he said in perfect Tumbuka.

Like the true missionary he was, he said a few words of comfort to grandma, said a prayer and left after a little while as the villagers began to assemble and mourn this person that had arrived only a short while ago from Harare.

Late that afternoon, I purchased some planks from the carpenter at the mission station and, giving him some approximate measurements, I watched him put together grandpa's coffin.

Once it was ready, I hired the Hospital's ox-drawn cart to transport the coffin home.

That night, I tried to keep to myself but the old men of the village kept drawing me to the fireside where they told stories and shared some jokes.

How on earth could they joke at a time like this?

Didn't they see that I was hurting?

I just wished they would have left me alone.

Now I understand why they did all that. Left alone, I probably would have done something real dumb, maybe even attempt to commit suicide. In a way, they were trying to draw me out of my shell, trying to divert my attention from that gripping pain that I felt inside me.

I could not go to sleep at all. I spent the whole night up, a lump stuck in my throat.

In the morning, the women went about cleaning the corpse and dressing it up in a garment they had sewn during the night from some material I had purchased the previous day.

Late in the afternoon, I led the procession from the house to the burial plot of the Gumbo clan, under the *mkhaya* tree. There in the mid afternoon March sun, I made the first mark on the ground, beginning the excavation of what would be grandpa's final resting place. I broke down, tears running down my face in a torrent.

With the assistance of the villagers, everyone taking turns at digging, the hole got deeper and deeper and, at last, using two ropes at either end of the coffin, we lowered it into the yawning ground and covered it with fresh earth.

23

A part of me was gone, forever, and no one could ever replace it, never.

After burying grandpa, despite the constant company with grandma, I became so disillusioned that I could not even concentrate on my work at the hospital. And Dr. Irvine had died while in Scotland and, Dr. Watts had gone back to Northern Ireland too.

It seemed all my support group I had relied upon was leaving me one way or the other. It felt like a part of me was missing, as if a vital cog had been removed from a piece of well oiled machinery.

I just could not get myself to function properly no matter how hard I tried to bring myself to terms with the situation. Each time thoughts of grandpa ran through my mind, tears would stream down my face and I would go into long periods of sobbing.

My grandfather, my dad and my best, friend was gone forever and all he had left me with was a legacy of love, of knowing how to care and share, to forgive and, most of all, to be patient, very patient with other people.

I could notice grandma observing me quietly and, somehow, she understood what I was going through, for she alone knew how extremely close I had been to the old man.

Strangely, she seemed to cope with the loss better than I did. Maybe she had known for a long time that this was bound to happen and she had sort of braced herself. At times when we sat down to have our evening meals, she would broach the subject of my going back to Zimbabwe so I could get myself a better job.

I reminded her that as there was a war going on, it was not possible for me to get back there and, besides, I argued, I could not leave her alone with no means of income.

The next eighteen months saw us grow closer to each other than we had been before. With my meager earnings from my job as Hospital Administrator *(The hospital relied on grants and donations from overseas donors and from PHAM in order to function)* we managed to survive from day to day.

However, when Zimbabwe attained its independence, the subject of my going back to Zimbabwe came up once more.

So, when my best friend and cousin, Perani Ziba, came to visit from Bulawayo, we made arrangements for me to go back with him. In January of 1981, I terminated my services with the Hospital.

I had had the honor of being appointed the first black Administrator and together with Dr. Watts, had been responsible for overseeing and approving plans and sketches of the new Hospital.

I promised grandma that as soon as I was settled down, I would come back for her so she could live with me.

Wishing her well, I finally left the village that had been home for the past four years and headed back to the land of my birth, Zimbabwe.

All my expectations and dreams came to naught. I did not know what fate had in store for me. As busy as I was trying to plan for grandma to come join me, some stronger forces had their own plans in motion already.

Little did I know that time was not on my side. About a year later, when my biological mother went visiting, we gave her some money and presents to give to grandma. We figured the money would see her through the rainy season until one of us next went to visit.

It so happened that after Fainess left Ekwendeni temporarily so as to visit my step dad's relatives, a person broke into grandma's house at night while she lay in bed and axed her, striking several blows to her head and leaving her to bleed to death.

After ransacking the house, all he managed to get away with was a National Bank of Malawi savings bank book and about thirty kwacha in cash.

Grandma had deposited all the money Fainess had given her into her savings account the previous day.

Her body was discovered two days later by some concerned neighbour.

And so, with none of her immediate family around, she was buried next to her husband in the Gumbo burial lot under the *mkhaya* tree.

So, when you, by any chance, happen to be passing through Ekwendeni 1 village and see two lonely graves by the *mkhaya* tree, please say hello to my grandma and grandpa, and say a prayer for me.